Dark Psychology and Manipulation

How to Stop Being Manipulated Without Needing to Go to Therapy. Find out the Secrets of Emotional Intelligence, Behavioral Psychology, and Cognitive Techniques

Anthony Secrets

Table of Contents

Chapter 4: How to Recognize Manipulators 44

Introduction

Congratulations for downloading **Dark Psychology Manipulation Book** and thank you for doing so. The following chapters will be discussing manipulation and ways in which politicians and religious leaders use manipulative techniques to make their followers stick with them to the end without suspecting anything. It discusses the various ways in which you will be able to recognize people who are manipulative and the manipulative techniques that they may use on you.

I am well aware that there are very many books that talk about this subject in the market but I am really grateful that you choose to read this one. Am sure you will enjoy every bit of it since every subject is discussed comprehensively. Please enjoy!

Why manipulation?

We live in a society that has very many selfish individuals. These are people who thrive through manipulation of the people around them. It is quite unfortunate that religious leaders and even politicians are in this category. They have turned to be manipulative to the people they are supposed to be showing the right direction. It is therefore important for the people in the society to be vigilant in order to ensure that they do not fall prey to such leaders. It should be the duty of every leader to ensure that they protect the people they have been entrusted with and offer the right guidance. Leaders in the church and also politicians are urged to remain loyal to their followers in order to ensure that they make the world a better place for them where they can live in peace and harmony.

Chapter 1: History of Manipulation

Manipulation has been experienced in many parts of the world. The first manipulative act was experienced in Europe in 400 BCE. Many manipulative interventions have been put in place but people have not been able to get away from it fully. Most politicians use manipulative skills to their political advantage. Even though the manipulation of people by their leaders is a universal politician and religious leaders have been known to be the most affected when it comes to manipulation. History states that manipulation was rampant in the 20th century mostly in America. One example is when Lincoln and Douglas would have heated debates when debating on the amendment of equal human rights bill in Virginia State.

Rikers described politics something that most political leaders use to manipulate their juniors. This was perfect since, through the debates, they would lure people to their side especially if they happen to win the debate. They try to show how powerful they are by making sure they win the debate. Those who do not win would normally play the victim and try to narrate their side of the story. Through these debates, most political followers were able to manipulate their followers and make sure that they remain faithful to them.

Many leaders have been known for their manipulative tactics on their followers. These leaders are not only politicians but also religious leaders. They are said to use emotional pleas and propagandas as well as populism in order for them to be able to manipulate the people they are expected to lead. Most politicians were said to use fear on their followers in order for them to be able to support some of their policies which they would not support in their normal self. Most leaders knew that their followers were illiterate so they would not understand anything. This made it easy for politicians to manipulate them even without their knowledge.

When the politicians instill fear in their followers, they will not most likely be able to overcome it because they do not have any power to do it. This made it for the politicians to manipulate them since they were dependent on them. Politicians were well aware that when their supporters remain dependent on them, they would not have any power over them. They would use lies and false promises to lure as many followers as possible into their circle. They would use all kinds of tactics in order to ensure that they follow them faithfully. There are those who would convince them to vote for a particular person whom they had a personal interest in.

The leaders would also use the past history to map the problems they would be facing at that time which their followers to believe that it was a cycle that was repeating itself. Communication empires would-be built-in order for them to be able to set the political agendas that they wanted. This would work to their advantage since they would spread the word to everyone around them which in return, they would get many supporters.

The politicians were very clever and still are. This is because they would strategize and come up with ways of ensuring that their followers do not exit from their group. They would, therefore, evoke fear amongst themselves which would make them stick with their leaders. They would also make sure that they strengthen their bonds in order for them to be able to deliver their messages without experiencing any challenges. They would even tailor messages which would be tailored for a specific audience. This would really work well for them since the audience would in return influence more people to join their leaders.

The leaders would also attack the leaders in the opposition. They would work tirelessly to make sure that they win as many people from the opposition to their side by attacking their leader through lies and propaganda.

We can all agree that most leaders use manipulation in order for them to have control over their followers. You will discover that the politicians know their target when they want to manipulate people. They make sure that their target is mostly on people who are vulnerable. For one to become a victim of a predator, they most likely have low self-esteem which makes them lack confidence in themselves. They would then make use of their weaknesses to manipulate them into any direction they would want them to follow.

It is not only the politicians who were known to manipulate people in the past. Various religious leaders would also manipulate their followers. Religious leaders used manipulation in the past so as to win people into their various religions. They inserted influence over them or maybe a group of followers in a clever way. They would make sure that their followers believed only in them. They would discover new strategies to lure their followers every often. This made the followers keep following them without questioning anything.

Religious leaders used manipulation in the past to win people into their various religions. They inserted influence over them or maybe a group of followers in a clever way. The same manipulation was passed down to the children by their parents. Parents manipulated their children by promising them to reward if the obey what they said and followed. In places of work, the bosses could manipulate the junior staffs by instilling cameras in the offices to monitor what they did at work by either practicing the religion or not. Severe punishment was given to those who did not practice religion at any given time. From the two incidences, you will find that people could follow blindly when pressure and intimidation are exerted.

Religion knows how to manipulate people cleverly. For instance, promising the followers eternal life after they die plus more blessings if they follow what is expected of them. Religion could limit people to think and to express their emotions because of the strict rules and dire consequences if they fail to follow the strict rules. People in religion were caged because it acted as a tool to manipulate and control them. It kept the oppressed silent and to obey what is said without objecting. They also did not have a say in the church. Theirs was to follow instructions failure to which they would have to go through the consequences of their disobedience.

Those who were stricken by poverty and diseases or those living in difficult life turned to religion to seek solace. They believed that their leaders would be able to help them with a good heart. They were not aware that they were just pretenders with their own interests. This made it easy for the leaders to manipulate their followers since they would only provide them with basic needs and they would sing to their tune. There are also those who would get into the religion to be taught how they should live because they were living an aimless life. Religion gave them a firm foundation on which they built their lives or so they believed.

The following are ways in which religion manipulated people: they depended on the religion where they are taught the principles of being righteous and walking in holiness. This teaching takes part when followers are very young. The principles will tie them from tender age till they become adults. Most of the concepts dealt with honesty, kindness, and love. They were taught that Jesus loved them so much. "Jesus loves little children." The loving image of Jesus is what makes children want to please Jesus as well. They were taught to commit their bodies and souls for glorification. If they fail, they will miss out heaven. They were taught that all the money they have, property and everything they owned is all in vain if they don't use it to grow the religion. When such teachings got into their head, they will lose control of their life. People started trusting everyone who could use religious phrases in their speech. You could find people abandoning their families and leaving their jobs so that they could get enough time to be a follower. Or they have gotten directions from God through their religious leaders. This made them even more miserable since they would not be able to even meet their needs. They had no otherwise but to keep following their religious leader who now properly manipulate them.

The leaders were also known for instilling the image of seeing God, heaven, and hell. This was to keep their message in line. For some, they could torture the followers with death and the consequences the will face in the second world. They could tell the followers if they wanted to move to the highest point in the kingdom. The person was to get married in the temple, mosque or church depending on the religion. They will arrive with the spouse and they will be given blessings of living eternally. This will exert pressure to ensure that their spouses are on the right track in terms of salvation.

The manipulated members could start branding individuals who could not believe in any doctrine that they were evil and glorious themselves that they were holy. For some, they could treat people horribly because they were going to pay their religious leaders and their sins could be cleansed.

They pretended to be alright though they needed help desperately because they wanted to prove how powerful the God they were serving. They were brainwashed to the point where they could not follow the modern medication for instance. When one was sick, he could talk of the miraculous god was going to heal them. They ended up dying miserably.

They stopped caring for people because they saw that they were holy than others. For instance, the scenario where we have both sexes marrying each other they called that evil. That was considered a sin. In a situation where a sister divorces his husband, they could not welcome her back home. They could refuse to accommodate her because of the sinful act.

Could religion be a world conspiracy? It is true because religious leaders have failed to produce proof of its authenticity. They only strive to make people believe in religion. They also insist on complying with the word and no one should question the bible because you will be considered a non-believer. The fact could be they have no room to think about religion. That could be enough to prove that they have been manipulated in believing. Religious leaders had mastered several tactics on how to win many followers into religion. Some of the tactics that they employed were they could speak loudly and preach with authority. That instilled fear in the followers.

Religion manipulation stretched its borders into government leadership. It was deep rotted in the most constitution in the world. The religious leaders could take part in the process of the constitution. That is why matter such as abortions is found in the constitution. Issues to do with sexuality debates, government offices closed due to holy days even to individuals who don't subscribe to those religions. The religious leaders forced the government into such matters. Issues to do with peacekeeping and reconciliation. Reconciliation is not wrong but coercing people to sign an agreement.

Could it be religion was seen as a business? Love for money can be a reason that manipulation is taking place. The big the number of followers the more the amount of money collected. From the study conducted in the United States of America, it was found out that religion was an industry that produced$ 1.2 trillion that year the report was conducted. From that report, you can deduce that people have invested in building their places of worship so that they can pocket a good amount of money. They even employ the staff members to serve the Lord.

With some other nations, you could find that in their places of worship they are busy running a business. They will open up faith- school-based and will be able to make an extra coin from it. They easily convince the followers that they are doing it to glorify God. The followers will move fast in bring money to the church because they feel they must develop their places of worship. Parents end up being manipulated because he thinks that if his child ends up in faith-based school. They will come out of there when they are a better person.

There is no religion that is not manipulative; individuals have distorted the meaning of religion to serve their selfish interests. They have introduced their own rules and doctrines. Many actions of violence are done in the name of religion. They offer structured teachings and learning, monitoring the followers strictly and ensuring they adhere to the set rules. They also plant fear in their hearts and mind so that they won't think of making a mistake or breaking the set rules and commandments.

Politicians and religious leaders aim were to make sure that none of their followers made it to a state where they can become independent. They had to remain poor in order for them to be able to manipulate them easily. Manipulation was, therefore, a tool that was greatly used and it is still being used by the leaders for the purposes of manipulation. With time, people started discovering themselves and started discovering that they were being manipulated so those who were determined to get away from the religion moved while others were left behind.

There are people who were totally brainwashed and so they could not be able to get away from their leaders. This lead to making them feel helpless and hopeless since they had no one to turn to. It also lowered their self-esteem and self-confidence. They would also not be able to communicate with the people around them freely since that's how religion and politicians have taught them.

Researchers have discovered that the reason why manipulators manipulated their followers is that they also wanted the things that their followers wanted. The only way to get them was to ensure that they lie to them and take everything and keep to themselves. This would enable them to make sure that their followers are dependent on them hence remain faithful followers to them.

You realize that most of the manipulator's words do not match what they do. They normally make sure that they tell you all the things you would want to hear. This applied to the manipulators in the past too. They would make sure that their followers only hear what they wanted to hear. When they were hungry, they would promise them food and money. They would also promise them eternal life if they obeyed. Through the promises, they had the chance to do everything they wanted with them. They, therefore, had an easy time manipulating them which would be for their selfish gain. Leaders in the past were therefore just like the current ones. Their main aim is to take everything and leave their followers desperately begging them.

Chapter 2: Politicians and Religions

How Politicians and Creators of Religion use Manipulative Techniques to make their Followers Believe in what they want

Manipulation can be described as anything that has the ability to influence individuals or groups of people whether it is through in a clever way or in a dishonest manner. Religious leaders have succeeded in using religion to manipulate their followers by promising them that they will enjoy life even after they die. They do this by limiting people thinking and controlling their emotions through their teachings and even issue them with consequences they are likely to face for not following the given instructions. This instills fear in them which makes them follow their leaders religiously.

Religious leaders are aware that their followers would love to good things to happen to them. They therefore deceptive language which makes them believe that they will achieve the things they wish to have if they follow them faithfully. The religious leader makes false promises to their followers which make them remain hopeful. They will also remain faithful to their religious leaders hoping that they will reap from their patience.

The followers are therefore forced to do things that when in their normal self they wouldn't do. It is true that we all have different views about our religion since we all belong to different religions that have different beliefs. For a long time, people have been judged depending on their religions. This is because, in as much as we have different beliefs, some can be manipulative. We may all call ourselves Christians but the things we do are of the world.

Most religious leaders have succeeded in manipulating Christians because they have the ability to manipulate the verses in their bible to suit the crowd they are talking to. They have been able to use their own views to communicate a message in the bible which makes it easy for their followers to believe in them. The followers are first brainwashed into believing that it is only their leader who can translate the word until it becomes meaningful to them.

When people's minds are wired that way, they blindly follow their religious leaders even when they know very well that the leaders do not have the best interests in their minds for them. This is because they have been forced to support leaders who do not qualify to be called religious leaders. They are also not allowed to go against their wishes as they have been made to believe that they may get curses from the disobedience.

The religious leaders also have the power to set rules that they expect all their followers to follow. They set the rules in accordance with the bible. They translate the rules to their followers and make them believe that they are from the bible. The leaders make sure that the rules are in their favor. This way, they will be able to manipulate them in whichever direction that they would like.

Religion has been greatly used by people to manipulate their fellow believers. It has been used to divide people by making them believe in different things. Religious leaders use various ways in order for people to understand a thing in their way. The followers will find themselves being submissive to their authorities. The leaders twist the word of God and use a language that is not fully understood by its followers. They will then use the teachings in their favor so the followers submit to them and follow and do everything that their leaders ask them to do.

The religious leaders use the word of God to commit some crimes which they later justify by stating that God controls everything. The followers will not suspect anything since they will be lead to believe that it is through God's will that everything happened. By doing this, the leaders are able to control as well as manipulate people in their society without them suspecting anything. Religious leaders are also known for using religious myths which are said to be a very powerful tool used since it is a psychological basis upon which all the other myths are known to flourish in.

The leaders use the myths to mobilize people who they later use to affirm the things they teach the people in the society. This way, anyone who goes against the rules and teachings is met with rejection from all the other believers. The believers are tuned to only believe and follow everything they are taught by the religious leaders. The leaders, therefore, use the word, believes and myths to manipulate their believers. When one is religiously manipulated, they are said to lose their ways through the following ways.

They stop seeing people for who they are. When you discover that you no longer see people as you used to see them, you will realize that there is a problem. When you start judging them depending on their religion then you have already been manipulated religiously as a person. This is because one has different believes about different things which have been forced down their throats by their religious leaders. This makes one start disliking the people around them since you according to you, everything they do is a sin.

The religion manipulation makes the people be too trusting especially to the people who incorporate their religion in their speech. There are those who even abandon their families and follow their spiritual parents. This is modern-day slavery since the followers will always follow what their followers say. They will follow them religiously stating that they are following the voice of the lord which was spoken to them through their leaders.

The religious leaders also lower their follower's self-esteem and confidence by ensuring that they do not have any powers. They are therefore made to become dependent on them such that they cannot make any decision on their own. They have to consult their leaders who most often are not truthful or honest to them. This makes it difficult for the followers to progress in any way since they have been fully controlled by their religion.

The followers will also most of the time be desperate since they have been taught not to speak up on matters concerning them. They will most times keep quiet even when they are experiencing any kind of problem since they have been taught to prove that their beliefs can help them in solving their problems. These are people who will even not go to the hospital when they are sick since their religion has taught them that they can get healed miraculously which in return makes them suffer in pain and some even die in the process.

The religious leaders also manipulate their followers into believing that anyone who does not have the same beliefs as them is evil. They will most times see themselves as holy since they have been blinded to think that way. These are leaders who have the power to extort money from their followers since they are only required to come up with a convincing story that the followers will believe. They are even told that they need to give all their money to be cleansed which they will follow and do blindly. All their sweat, therefore, end up with their spiritual fathers.

Politicians have also not been left behind in manipulating their followers to believe what they want them to believe. It has been noted with a lot of concern that politicians have power and money to lure and brainwash their followers into making them believe in them and keep them around just for them to be used. These politicians are aware that their followers are gullible and so, it would not be a difficult thing to win them to their side. The followers, on the other hand, believe that politicians have solutions to all their problems. That's why it is so easy to manipulate them. Below are some of the manipulative techniques that the politicians use on their followers.

Altruism

This is referred to as the methods that the politicians use to brainwash their followers into making any sacrifices for them without giving it much thought. Politicians use their magic to ensure that the followers believe in them in order to lure them into their circle. Most followers trust easily. They believe that politicians are really powerful and that they cannot let them down. They would be willing to do anything in order to ensure that their politicians are happy.

The followers will, therefore, be ready to do anything for the politicians. These followers will, therefore, be ready for war if asked to and will do anything to make sure that their political leaders are happy. This is because their minds have been wired to feel that it is their responsibility to protect their leader from any harm. The leaders, therefore, benefit from manipulating their followers without any effort.

Money

Most politicians know that people poor and would be happy and follow them religiously if given some little money. They, therefore, use the money to corrupt people's minds and make them follow and even elect them without questioning anything. The politicians will always give money that is not even enough for the followers to meet their needs. The followers will, therefore, keep coming back to them for more tokens. The little money they are given is meant to act as a bribe into following them. They are also expected to lure more people into the side of the politicians who promises to give them money. This makes the followers believe everything that their leader tells them and they cannot go against anything that the politician tells them.

Sowing Seeds of Fear in People's Minds

Fear is considered to be one of the most powerful emotion that can be used to lure people to your side. When people are in fear, it is so easy to manipulate them. This is because they do not want to find themselves in situations that would threaten their lives. Politicians use this opportunity to make them follow them faithfully with promises of making the situations better.

Politicians use fear since it captures everyone's attention. This is because everyone will only focus on the things that are making them fear. Fear also makes people shut down their thinking. They will all be focusing on eliminating the things that may be causing them to fear. Most of them will be looking up to the politicians to solve all their problems. They will, therefore, be on the politician's side who may be promising them protection in return for their votes or any other favor.

Provoking People and Making them Angry and Hostile

When people's minds have been instilled with fear, they make it very easy for politicians to become hostile and angry. When in this situation, they only need to make up stories that people will believe and react to. This is a win on the politician's side since he will be pretending to put in efforts to bring solutions that are also in his favor.

Playing the Big and Strong Messiah to Your Followers

Most politicians play with their followers minds by making them believe that they are the only people who can solve all of their problems. They do this by making claims that are not realistic which the followers tend to believe. They make efforts to show that they are the only ones who are able while they only appear in the projects technically and leave which makes the followers think they are doing anything for them. They also win their followers by spoiling names for fellow politicians. They make the followers believe that those politicians cannot solve any of their problems. The followers will therefore only believe in their leader and follow them religiously and they will do everything they are told by the politicians without questioning.

Acting as the Superior Ones Among Their Opponents

Most of the politicians win people's attention by acting superior to all the politicians around them. There are people who feel good being associated with someone who is superior. These politicians will disobey their seniors and make their followers feel like they are untouchable. They make the other leaders feel like they don't deserve their time. The arrogance pulls a great crowd to their side since they feel like their leaders are so powerful. This helps a lot in making the followers believe in them. They will want to be associated with the untouchable politician who has solutions to all their problems.

Telling Lies

Politicians thrive in lies. They lie about almost everything as long as they are able to get the attention of their followers. The politicians will lie about helping their followers and make them believe that they will actually help them. They will, therefore, remain hopeful and keep following them. Whenever they are caught in scandals, they will deny and make their followers believe that they were not in any way involved. Their followers will keep defending them and following their instructions since they cannot detect any lies in the politician's statements.

Spinning the Truth

Many are times when politicians are accused of various things but they normally twist the facts to their favor.

They will be found in bad behavior but they will give a contradicting story which seems real in order for them to make their followers believe that they are clean. They justify their actions and make their followers believe that they were not involved in the scandals. The followers, therefore, continue being faithful believers of the politicians since they cannot see their faults.

Playing the Victim

Most politicians are known for playing the victim when they are found with mistakes. They find sympathy from their followers by making them believe that they cannot make such mistakes. They will even show false evidence that they are being accused of things that they did not do. This makes their followers believe them and continue believing in them.

Positive Support

The politicians may get faithful supports by buying presents and gifts. They even buy their children's uniforms and all the needs they need for schooling purposes. This will make the followers feel forever grateful to the politicians since they came through for them when they were in need.

It is important for people to learn and understand their religious leaders in order for them to ensure that they are not manipulated by them. There is a need to be able to tell when they are being manipulated. This will help them to avoid the manipulative leaders and embrace the honest and leaders who have their best interests at heart. Knowing the leaders to associate with will make the world a better place. Leaders will also learn to work for the people without expecting anything in return. By doing this, they will be able to handle their followers with respect and not only use them for their political and religious gain.

Chapter 3: The Secrets of Emotional Intelligence

Emotional intelligence today has become a very important skill in every sector. Starting from the place of work to the community you come from. This skill is all about how you present yourself when around people, how you can offer them help when they need help when things are not working as expected do you just sit or you exercise a little patience. That is the reason the skill is becoming more important in every sector. At work for instance when seeking a promotion nowadays they don't consider your technical skill. They look deep into your interpersonal skills. So, if you are about to be promoted work on your interpersonal skills to show to your boss that you also afford them.

We all have individuals either at the place of work or in our neighborhood, which are good at listening to people. No matter the incident you are in, they always have something to say and how to say it. What they say doesn't disappoint or offend at all. They are always caring and understanding. At some point when we don't find a solution to the problem but we will leave his place feeling much better and hoping to find a solution soon.

When you are stressed, how do you manage your emotions? We have people are masters when it comes to managing their own emotions. Such an individual doesn't get upset in stressful situations. They can look into problems and calmly find a solution. They are good at making decisions and know when to trust their conscience. Regardless of their strengths, they know how to look at themselves with honest. They take criticisms well and when they can use it to improve their performance. Such individuals have a high degree of emotional intelligence. They know themselves better plus their needs.

People have different personalities, achievements, wants and different ways of showing their emotions. We were all created differently. Emotionally intelligent people can recognize their own emotions and know they affect people around them. It also involves how you perceive people and managing relationships more effectively. Individuals with more emotional intelligence are always successful in the thing they do. The reasons are they play as team players, they also make others feel good and they see life in a positive dimension.

Being in Control of Pressure

A person with emotional intelligence can be in a position to handle his emotions when there is more pressure. Pressure can be from a relationship or at the place of work. Or any other case in which we can have pressure at times. Everyone at any given time in life we face pressure. But with the right remedy, we can handle it without letting it get out of hand. As responsibilities increase to pressure and command. A person with emotional intelligence will stay calm and keep all his feelings in order and will not react spontaneously to any crisis. You need to show to your boss that you can handle hard situations in a calm manner. If your juniors staff report an issue to you need to give the assurance that you will be in a position to handle and the situation will get back to normal.

Listening to Others

The secret to emotional intelligence is being in a position to listen to others. How do you listen? You will listen to them in a way that will make them feel that they were heard. One way of dealing with the crisis at the place of work is by making individuals feel that whenever they have complained they are heard. That is why it is important to hire managers who will be good listeners. When someone has an idea or advice even if they won't implement right away but at least they had to listen to his idea. One motivating factor to the staff is when they get a manger that gets to listen to them and understand them. They will strive to achieve the best for the company. They also feel that they are part of the company.

Empathizing

If you are that person who shows empathy to others then you have the secret of emotional intelligence. We all have a life outside our offices or places of work. Some married with children but still you will find they have challenges here and there. Those in a relationship may break up and may need someone to advise them that those are part of life. Our family members and close friends may fall sick and other situations may affect us. If you have the best boss then he should help you overcome whatever you are facing. No technical skill is required for your boss to show you empathy. He will be human and sensitive to help you in a hard week instead of leaving you hungry and sending you to the streets to look for a new job.

Owning Up Mistakes

They will take up responsibility when there is a mistake in the company. Those people with emotional intelligence will not see themselves as failures but a powerful mindset that is ready to be a great leader in the future. Nobody likes failures and negative feedback. People who accept corrections even from the junior staff members are a great leader. It helps them to learn and improve faster. Those who fear to be criticized don't take the initiative of trying out something new. Even though the criticisms may not have landed correctly but gives you an idea of how other people think. Next time you make a mistake own it up and try to rectify before it gets out of hand. That is what is done by intelligent managers.

Being Open-Minded

An open-minded person is a good leader. They keep their ego on point and take criticisms positively. They know that having constructive criticisms will help them improve on leadership skills. Make sure you always strive to improve a situation. Even if there is minimal improvement. Always be open to feedback because companies are always willing to give promotions to employees who seek feedback. They see that such people have an interest in growing the company and don't risk their credibility. Whenever critique by your boss takes it positively. When you receive negative feedback, are calm and ask yourself how the situation is going to make you better. See to it that he had good intentions of doing that.

Solving Conflicts

In place of work, we have different kinds of people. We have those who like to fight when they are wronged and those who are so silent even when offended. Conflict is bound to happen because we will differ in opinion. Being a manager means you will have to deal with conflicts. They will be reported to your desk. Effective managers will have to deal with the situation without getting emotionally involved in the conflict. They should look for common ground and listen to the stories from both sides. Though in other instances it will not be easy but will have to show that you are an effective mediator.

Respect

Respect is earned when you respect other people. It is two-way traffic. You will earn others respect if you will be doing the right thing and at the right time and place. Individuals who are always calm and able to control their emotions have time to listen to others and treat everyone fairly will earn the respect of others. They don't force them to respect him or control and draw attention for the sake of respect. The emotional intelligent people are always approachable. They see that their role is helping others to succeed. If you incorporate all these skills in your endeavors you go far.

Being Aware of Our Emotions

Self-awareness is also a secret to emotional intelligence. Without self-awareness then it means you are blind. You cannot go anyway because you can't see. You can evaluate yourself if you don't have self-awareness. You cannot know what you have and what you lack and what you need to acquire. When you have self-awareness, you will be in a position to understand one's deep emotions, their strengths, and weaknesses, needs and achievement and their passion. Individuals with self-awareness are always honest to themselves and others. They also recognize how people around them feel and the effects of those feelings. Do you see yourself as an accurate person? What if your friends? To start with yourself you will rate yourself as not an accurate person same case to your friends. We should learn to compliment ourselves for any achievement plus what we have not achieved.

Controlling Our Emotions

We at some point have very emotional people around us. If we can regulate our emotions then we are emotionally intelligent. Those individuals who are wise don't and rashly respond thing or you find them acting without thinking. It is an easy theory but you will find that is difficult for people to practice. This will save you from embarrassments and hasty decisions. The emotionally intelligent take their time and find out what could have gone wrong before responding to things. Being in control of your thoughts you don't become a slave to your emotions. By doing that you will stay in harmony with your goals and achievements. Something, once you have reached there, is no reverse gear for them that is why it advisable you take your time in all cases. Individuals who know how to regulate their emotions make better decisions. They are more flexible and act with a lot of truthfulness. They are always mindful of others.

Motivation and Achievements

Are you the kind of person who gets motivated by external factors? External factors are the big salary that you earn or the status quo that comes with a big title at work or working for a big company that is well known worldwide. A person with emotional intelligence will only be motivated by the achievements they make to the company and the people he is working for. The best way to track your achievements is by writing down what you have in a day. Keep records of all your achievements it will become easy to track them down.

Socialization

Do you mingle with people easily and make friends? Does that friendship last? All human beings are social animals. They can mingle and make several friends. Social skill is one of the emotional intelligence skills. Having that ability to build and able to have good rapport in the relationship that you have built. You will be in a position to manage friendship if you understand and try to manage your emotions. Being in the shoes of others. Being optimistic in whatever situation, when things are not right you still have the motivation to move on.

Being Remorseful

We all do mistakes at some point in life. But is it wise to ask for forgiveness when we have done a mistake? A good number of people find it hard to ask for forgiveness. It will only take the strength and guts to be able to say sorry. Asking for forgiveness does not mean you were wrong but it shows how humble you are and with a lot of humility. When we ask for forgiveness it makes other people admire what we have. People who value friendship more than their ego asks for forgiveness.

Forgiving and Forgetting

Many of us have been held hostage by our emotions. We forgive but we don't want to forget. No matter how big the mistake was we should learn to forgive and forget. It is something that has holds several people back, why?

When you are held hostage, you won't move but you will always be thinking of what that particular person did to you. It is like inserting your finger into boiling water and leaving it there instead of removing it. That finger will never heal. The offending person moves on with her own life. You should forgive and forget to allow you to heal and it will prevent others from enslaving your emotions.

Rewarding and Appreciation

We all love to be acknowledged or praised when we do well. It builds our self-esteem. This is achieved when we focus on the good things in others. That is why you will find in schools when releasing exams, the award the best performed in that particular exam. This is a form of appreciating the good work done. This will be a motivating factor for that student to continue working hard. Those who were not rewarded will be motivated to work hard next time so that they can be appreciated as well.

Offering Help

Helping others is the greatest way of caring emotions of others. Most people don't care knowing if you are going through hard situations or not. Do they have that time to offer help in the first place? They are always busy with their schedules. They run up and down without knowing who their next neighbor is. People now days don't know the person who he leaves next to. This is being irresponsible. You can imagine sparing some of your time and getting to help those who need help it will be a good show for them. Actions of that kind will build their trust and you will make others to follow your lead. Emotional intelligence has a dark side. When people attempt to joke around with you or want to pick a fight with you. How will you protect yourself? You will only overcome this if you are intelligent in dealing with such rascals. They are not after something better. Theirs is to cause trouble to others. You need to know how to deal with them as someone with emotional intelligence.

Dedication and Commitment

Have you ever agreed with someone he fails to turn up? Many people are fond of breaking up agreements and commitment when they feel like doing it. Imagine a scenario where you had promised your daughter to take her out on a weekend. Then you failed to show up. Imagine how the small girl will feel? She will see you as a bad person who does not honor the promises he makes. The next you promise her something she will not trust that you are going to fulfill it. Same case to those who don't honor agreement such people are never committed. We have people who like to stick to their words. They mean what they say and they see value and principles in what they say. The main reason for sharing is because you want them to learn something from it. Not all people will appreciate what you have shared with them. Those who see sense will be ready to listen and won't have meetings later your thoughts and feelings.

In conclusion, emotional intelligence makes one aware of his actions and feelings. They also look into how they affect the people around them. When looking into people around it means you value them. You get to listen to what they want or their needs being able to care for them at different levels. Emotional intelligence is becoming a very important skill because it helps you to relate well with others and makes you achieve your goals. That is why companies now days test emotional intelligence of people before hiring them

Chapter 4: How to Recognize Manipulators

Have you ever felt that someone is controlling you, be it in a relationship when your partner does not give you room to express yourself? He only acts without informing you. You only find out later that certain thing was done. You could be manipulated by your partner. Manipulative individuals try to control others. There are different forms of manipulation. It can be from an abusive partner, your boss at work and not forgetting the salesperson. It is easy to identify manipulative people. How will you know that this person is manipulative? Some of the manipulative techniques they use are:

They do away with your willpower. They create doubts or they sow doubt in you so that you will remain in their protection. You will not have an opportunity to decide on your own. They do away with your ability to trust yourself and disable your justification.

They also destroy your self-esteem. They get rid of everything you have achieved. They do criticize by only highlighting the negative sides. They work to distort and do away with your sense of reality.

They don't represent reality. They only enjoy when they create confusion by creating arguments and misunderstanding among individuals. After they generate dispute the sit and watch how people are fighting one another as they laugh.

How Do You Feel When You are the Subject of Manipulation?

This is about individuals who use certain manipulation techniques. The techniques they use are meant to create confusion and anguish to the point that you don't trust yourself or your mind plus your own decisions. As much as they are always around us it is not easy to notice these individuals. Because no one carries a sign in their forehead indicating that he or she is a manipulator.

 When manipulated you will feel that you are full of fear, guilty and obligated. This because you are being coerced to do something that you don't want to participate in. you will feel scared in doing it but you will be obligated to do it and you will be guilty if you fail to do it. A manipulator, in other words, can be a person who bullies you because he may end up using threats, intimidating you and using violence so that he can instill fear in you.

Why Avoid Such People?

Such people nourish in the throbbing of others. They make you feel that you are guilty or you cannot trust anything after a certain situation. They create an impression in you whatever he has said is correct and there should be no reason to object.

Do You at Some Point Ask Yourself Questions?

A manipulator may make you ask yourself a lot of questions. The question may be based on realism, remembrance, and your feelings. A manipulator may twist what you said and make it suit them. They may also take be in charge of your discussion and create a scenario that you will feel that you have said something wrong to them. At that point, you may try to defend yourself or you will become guilty. You will feel that you have completely offended them.

Have You Ever Had Someone Offering to Do a Favor for You?

If one does a favor to you, remember it is not for free. There is something that the person is targeting. He is trying to manipulate you. He is only trying to be nice to you. At that time, you may be confused because you need help you won't think of the other side of the help. But the moment you fail to meet the expectation of the manipulator you will realize that he was trying to exploit you. Because he makes sure that you are made unappreciative in the scenario. A good example of this manipulation is in a relationship. A partner may buy you a gift, for example, a wristwatch or may decide to take you out for lunch or dinner. After all that he request for a favor in return. This is abusing the social standard. It is good to give in return for special treatment but in some instances, some favors are not sincere.

Not all people who behave that way are trying to manipulate you. For some, it is the way they behave. It is good to know such behaviors in the case when your safety and rights are at stake you report the matter to the concerned authority.

Shifting the Goal Post

In a scenario, you are trying to argue out you stand and trying very hard to give your reasons they shift their goal post to fix you and tell you that they are not satisfied with your response. This is the time you will fumble and try to look for all evidence in the world to set you free.

Changing the Topic

Have you ever been in a conversation then all of a sudden someone new joins you in that discussion then all of a sudden, the topic of discussion is changed? Master manipulator does that and pretends to be innocent. Manipulators do that so as that they may not be held accountable in case of anything.

Taking Advantage of Physical Space

A manipulator will insist on meeting up with you in his or her physical place. This will be a flat form of exercising domination and be in charge of the discussion. Space can be in his office, care home or any other place that will seem familiar to her or him.

They Give You the Chance to Speak First

By doing that he will be establishing your baseline and looking into your area of weakness.

This technique is mostly used by sales personnel. They do that by asking their customers inquisitive and all-purpose question to set up the baseline about your thoughts and manners. From the questions, they will be able to know your weaknesses and your strengths. This inquisitive questing can also take part in the place of work.

They Take Part in the Meaningless Dialogue.

You can imagine being in a conversation for more than ten minutes but what the manipulator is saying is nonsense. They give illogical explanations. When you see that they are dominating it is high time you cut the conversation short by leaving. Instead of them messing around with you.

The Exploitation of the Whole Story

Their main goal is to undermine your morale. They can put words in your mouth that you have not uttered. They will make you think that they can read your mind. But that is just a trick. The manipulator gets to change your own story. By giving false information about your own story. This may end up making you be angry with the manipulator and may want to pick a fight with him. They will try and victimize you. Their main agenda is to deform your character. They may also give an overstatement of your story which is a one-sided biased story.

Behave as if they are Most Knowledgeable

They make general and vague statements. Their achievement is to send away and damage your opinion. They give a general conclusion.

Some manipulators may behave as if they are intellectuals but in reality, they are formless. They pretend that they know more than you. They will do that by imposing records of information and details that you know little about. This can happen in the sales department or the monetary state. They presume power over you. The manipulator had his intentions of intimidating you with the ambiguous data. He eventually pushes through with his plan. You will be sited there convinced that facts never lie. In other scenarios, some individuals use this technique for other reasons.

Use Bureaucracy

This technique is used to delay the facts and the truth about a certain matter you were looking into. They will give procedures, rules, and regulations involved in the laws and has the committee to look into the issue. All these are to block you from assessing the facts. But for them, they will maintain their power and position while making your life more difficult.

Exhibiting Depressing Emotions

They will do that by increasing their voice as if shouting at you. This form of manipulation is called violent manipulation. They do that so that you can submit to their coercion and give them what they want. This manipulation is always accompanied by burly body language such as standing and use gestures that will have increased force.

Pessimistic Blows

They use this to set you off. By doing this they will gain an emotional advantage. This can be in the negotiation then suddenly to a profession. Of which you were not given time to prepare. Your presentation won't be perfect because you were ambushed. After that, you get negative comments but you won't be in a position to salvage yourself.

No Given Time to Make Decision

These negotiation tactics are mostly used by sales personnel. They put pressure on you to make a hasty decision before you change your mind. By doing that he will now be in control and you will award in easily to his order.

Using Humor

The humor they will use is negative. They are meant to thrust at your weaknesses and to make you powerless. This critical remark can be humorous or sarcastic. They can be in terms of your appearance, the old fashion clothes you have put own, the type of the phone you are carrying around. The bottom line of these criticisms is to make you look bad and also making you feel bad. They hope to have superiority over you.

Criticisms and Judgments.

This is a bit different from using humor. The manipulator uses criticism to create an impression that there is always something wrong with you. No matter how hard you try and please him you still become inadequate and he will never see something good in you. This happens to you yet he cannot give concrete evidence or does not provide a solution to all your shortcomings or ways to help you deal with them.

Being Silent

This is choosing not to pick any of your phone calls, not replying ant text messages, emails, and any other investigation. He does that so that he can make you wait or at some point creating doubts in your mind. They can ignore you when talking to them as a form of punishment. More so when you are the point on the need they push you away? When you try asking them something they will not speak.

Faking Ignorance

In this tactic, one pretends that he or she does not understand what you want. Or what you want her to do for you. He does that so that you can take his responsibility and work on whatever you wanted to be done. This mostly used by children when they don't feel like doing something. They delay themselves so that an adult can do that thing for them. The same tactic is also used by some adults as well. In cases when one is trying to hide something or they wish to avoid a certain task.

Tress Passing the Boundary Line

Tress passing your boundary line does not happen the moment you meet. He will first try to test what would be your reaction if she crosses your boundary line. When the boundary line is crossed and no retaliation it will lead to crossing another and another until it gets deeper. That is when they win up your mind and overpower you.

Dominating and Having Full Control

One major characteristic of manipulators is controlling. If they are around people you will find that they will issue threats so that they can be in control of everyone. They tend to be superior and hold others in bondage. When trying to dominate you will find that they will make their intentions known to everyone. If they don't succeed in dominating you will find that they will react and everyone becomes an enemy.

Attracting Guilt

The manipulator transfers his negative traits to another person. He even holds another person responsible for the mistake he did. He gives the blame with no reasons to prove it. This happens when the victim has a soft spot. Does not worry about trying to defend himself or herself. The manipulator gets away easily. The manipulators' intentions are his success and happiness. He does not worry about what the other person could have felt. They target the emotional weakness and how vulnerable the victim is. He then coerced the victim into yielding to his calls and command.

Victimization

The manipulator gives an exaggerated personal situation. This is to attract sympathy from the recipient.

He will talk falsely of his health that he has a condition that needs attention. He will pretend to be weak and has no power at all. The main reason he does that is to exploit people in terms of money and their time. People will exercise goodwill to see to it that he gets money so that he can get proper medication. People will feel guilty and see that they now must protect and nurture him. He will be extracted with no reason at all.

Marketing Their Character

Have you meet up with people who will talk so much about their personality before they are asked. They will only say good things about their personal life and their achievements so far. This technique is mostly used by politicians. They first identify what the person wands and they pretend they will meet those expectations but they have a target.

They Do a Lot of Gossiping

When the manipulators find it had to control you, they change their tactics. They will now focus on spreading false things about you behind your back. This will change how people will see you. At some point, they will start following you up and down. Monitoring every move, you make then they will start criticizing. The idea is to bring you down both emotionally and psychologically. For example, you are in a relationship with someone then you plan to break up because you have your reasons. They will go around propagating false information about the relationship. Instead of them finding out the true story behind the break up from you. They won't have that time because their main intention is to make you look like a bad person in the eyes of people. Who goes around breaking their hearts and betraying their trust?

In conclusion, emotional manipulation does not select a gender. Both male and female can be manipulative. It better that you have an insight into the tricks and tactics applied by these individuals. Manipulation is not a good experience for those who are practicing it. Those people are self-centered. They don't think about the welfare of others. You can prevent manipulation from spreading further by educating yourself or others about the negative impact it has on other peoples' lives. Share with them how to identify manipulative persons and the reason they should run away from them

Chapter 5: Advanced Techniques of Behavioral Psychology

Behavioral psychology is referred to as the study which shows the connection between one's mind and the behavior that they portray. Behavioral psychology enables therapists to be able to predict how people will behave which enables them to nurture better habits which will enable them to co-exist with each other without experiencing any kind of challenges.

People behave differently and their behavior may be influenced by the environment around them. They may have acquired their behavior from the people around them even though there are those behaviors that we inherit from our parents and other relatives. Good behavior can be nurtured when one falls in the right hands.

There are so many psychologists out there who have knowledge and skills nurturing better behavior in human beings. One is therefore required to engage a qualified therapist who will be of help in ensuring that they get their desired behavior. The psychologists that one chooses should have the knowledge and skills required to handle different behavioral cases.

People can also make use of the internet when they encounter psychological problems. They do not have to rely on counselors or therapists. There is a lot of information on YouTube and other sites which are helpful so people should ensure that they are making good use of them. One of the benefits of using the information on the internet is that it is free as long a one has internet access.

One can also access the information from anywhere. They do not have to be available for the therapies physically. It also saves them a lot of them since they do not have to rush in order for them to beat traffic for them to be at the place of appointment on time. Another benefit of sourcing for information from the internet is that they can do it at the comfort of their home or office. One does not have to get out of the house. However, for one to get help, they have to be disciplined with time in order for them to achieve the set goals. That's why it is advisable to engage a psychologist with a physical location in order for them to give proper guidance until you recover from the challenges that you may be facing.

Psychologists use behavioral techniques when they want to change people's behavior. The techniques work well for clients who are ready to change their behavior. The therapists work on finding the root cause of certain behavior and work on eliminating it. For example, when a therapist comes across a client who has a problem with alcohol, they look for the cause of the problem and try to eliminate it completely. They do not just treat the problem but also its cause.

Several techniques have been proven to work well in the elimination of the behavioral problems as well as the symptoms. I have discussed some of them below.

Systematic Desensitization

This therapy was discovered by a psychologist known as Joseph Wolfe who designed it specifically for people who have extreme phobias. People with extreme phobias may be very difficult to deal with. This is because they fear almost everything so the therapist has to ensure do trial and error until they find what works for them and what does not work for them.

This psychologist however discovered this treatment which is said to follow a process known as counter-conditioning. This means that the relationship between the stimulus and nervousness is made weak through the relaxation techniques and anxiety hierarchies as well as through desensitization. Below are some steps which he used in the process of systematic desensitization.

Step 1: Building a ladder of the anxiety arousing provocations which should include the extent of fear one experiences when they encounter various things. At this point, one lists everything that makes them aroused. They also state how they feel at the sight of those things.

Step 2: The spider is trained on how they are supposed to relax their muscles.

Step 3: The client is trained in ways of working through the hierarchy even as they use the relaxation technique. The psychologist will make sure that they discuss the various things that make the client anxious. They help the clients to be able to use the relaxation techniques.

Step 4: The client is taught on ways of ensuring that they overcome their anxiety on things that they fear. They are guided into facing their fears which helps them to be able to overcome them.

Exposure Therapies

The exposure therapy techniques are made in such a way that the client is exposed to situations that they fear. For example, if they fear snakes, they will be exposed to pictures of snakes, movies with snakes and so forth. The exposure to the things that they fear makes them get used to them and slowly learn to live with them. The situations are therefore said to provoke their situations which makes them get used to them with time.

The psychologist will normally introduce brief fearful situations and later introduce longer fearful situations. The client will, therefore, get used to them little by little which helps them to cope with them as time goes by. By being exposed to fearful situations, the client is able to adapt to seeing them every often so they will not have a challenge overcoming their fear and anxiety.

This therapy may however not work for everyone since there are those who will shut down once exposed to such situations. The counselor should, therefore, be able to find out what works for each client. This will help a lot in ensuring that the type of therapy used works for individual clients.

Flooding Technique

Flooding refers to a state of exposing a client to the actual or real situations which they fear or feel anxious about. They get exposed to them for long periods of time. For example, if a client fears spider, they can get exposed to the spiders for a long period of time. This will make them develop relaxation techniques to overcome their fear of spiders. They will, therefore, be able to stay in a room that has spiders longer the next time.

The client should, however, be educated about this kind of technique so that they get comfortable with it before they go through the process. This will help a lot in ensuring they do not become traumatized by the situations. A counselor should be in a position to tell the clients state of the mind before exposing them to any kind of situation. This will help in ensuring that they do not expose them to situations that would make the situation they are in even worse.

A wise counselor should be able to tell when to use this tactic and when to avoid it. This is because there are times that it would not work and there are those times when it works perfectly. There are clients who cannot get used to situations no matter which method is used. They will still be anxious about the situation. The therapist, therefore, needs to ensure that they find other ways other than exposing them to situations that will make them anxious.

The counselors can use their reactions to the things that make them anxious and find ways of making them overcome their anxiety. There are those people who may not react to the things making them anxious immediately. They react to them later so the flooding technique may not really work for them.

Aversion Technique

This is a technique which therapist use when they do not have any other option other than using it. They will use it when they are completely unable to help a client overcome their aversion behavior. It is a treatment which is carried out through comparing one's aversion behavior with the stimulus which may have a response that is not so desirable. This method is normally used in order for the therapist to reduce unwanted behavior. This method may have some great effects on the client hence the need to ensure that it is used as the last option.

Modeling Technique

Modeling is a technique that therapists use when they want to give treatment which involves the improvement of one's interpersonal skills. There are many people out there who are struggling with socialization. They do not know how to interact with others which makes them use the wrong approach which in the end causes conflicts with the people around them. This becomes a problem when they cannot control it. This technique is mostly used with people who have problems with communication and also those who encounter problems when it comes to interaction with people in a social setting. Techniques such as live modeling and role-playing as well as convert modeling and participant modeling are the most common modeling techniques used.

With live modeling, a client sits back and watches a model who may be a counselor modeling a certain behavior and they copy the behavior from them. They are expected to be very keen since they will be expected to model the exact behavior. The counselor models the behavior that they expect their client to acquire. This is why they are expected to practice it.

For role-playing, the counselor will normally role-play a certain behavior with the client which enables the client to practice the behavior. With the participant behavior modeling, the counselor first models the behavior they want the client to acquire, they then the client practices the behavior as the counselor models that same behavior. Lastly, convert modeling is when a counselor makes the client imagine somebody else performing the behavior. They do not need to watch anyone modeling the behavior.

Assertive Training

Assertive training is a technique that is used to help clients to be able to solve conflicts amongst themselves, to make realistic goals and also skills on management of stress. The therapist trains their clients on ways of ensuring that they overcome all kinds of pressures whether it is at their workplace or even in society.

Through assertive training, the counselors conduct training by engaging the trainees in the listing of the areas that they have difficulty in. this helps them to point out specific areas that a certain behavior keeps repeating itself which makes it easy for them to work on it. The clients are then lead in role-playing which helps them to experience the issues and find their solutions. Through assertive training, the clients are able to overcome their fears and anxiety issues since they have the confidence to try out new things which they believe they will be of help in solving the issues facing them.

Cognitive Behavior Technique

Cognitive behavior technique is normally used by therapists to help clients or patients to understand how their thoughts can influence their behavior. Therapists use it to treat phobias, anxiety and depression and many other disorders. This technique is used to help clients who may be encountering specific problems.

The patients are educated on the various ways of dealing with any kind of destructive behavior. They will be able to identify any changes in their behavior which may be influencing them negatively and be able to work on them. The main aim of cognitive behavior is to ensure that they are able to deal with most of the challenges they may be dealing with in their lives. They may not be able to deal with everything but they can try and be in control of most of the things that may be happening to them on their day to day activities.

Through cognitive behavior techniques, people are able to see things differently. This is because their brain has been wired to see things differently. One becomes thinks through things before doing them because they have developed rational thinking. They see things positively since they are in control of what goes on in their brain.

People are also able to control their thoughts. This means that they are able to stop any kind of thinking that is unwanted and concentrate only on important things. They are also able to think clearly and more rationally since they know the right and wrong things. They are also able to control their thoughts and are confident that all the decisions they make are valid. Confidence is built which in return makes people have high self-esteem.

Therapists are also said to use this therapy for the treatment of depression. Patients are able to get guidance little by little until when they get better. This is because the therapist introduces treatment that they are sure that it will work well with the patient. They also make sure that they find a permanent solution to the depression and any other kind of problem that one may be experiencing.

Positive Reinforcement

Positive reinforcement is when a counselor introduces a wanted behavior or even a pleasurable stimulus after a specific behavior has been detected. The desirable stimulus is meant to reinforce one's behavior which makes it definite that the behavior will recur. It is a method that is said to be very successful in ensuring that individuals acquire good behavior. Positive reinforcement is used for clients with behavioral problems. It helps them to be able to get the desired behavior. Whenever one shows an undesirable behavior, the undesirable stimulus normally introduced in order for the bad behavior to be discouraged.

The counselors may also introduce negative reinforcement. It is defined as a way in which one removes undesirable behavior in order for them to encourage a specific behavior. They can also use negative punishment by removing the removing a desirable stimulus in order for them to discourage certain behavior. All the reinforcements are useful in ensuring that all kinds of behaviors are managed.

Introduction of positive reinforcement is important in so many ways. One of them is that the therapist is able to reward an unpleasant behavior and ensure that it gives a positive outcome. When a sequence of behaviors is rewarded, the therapist is likely to get better results.

Reinforcing good behavior is helpful in ensuring that people open up to the people around them without fear. Through positive reinforcement, people are able to feel good about the choices they make in their day to day lives. They will always be feeling motivated to do better each day so that they get more rewards.

Positive reinforcement has been proven to improve the performance of the employees in their workplaces. This is because they are motivated and have confidence in themselves. They are therefore able to give their best which in return increases their productivity a work. Most of the stuff will also have desirable behavior while at work and even when they are at home. Their behavior becomes consistent which helps in ensuring that they do not go back to undesirable behavior. Positive reinforcement is therefore important and should be practiced in order for employers and employees to experience positive change at their workplace.

Chapter 6: Special Anti-Manipulation Techniques Used by Prisoners of War

Edward Hunter, an American journalist was the first person to raise alarm on what he termed as "brainwashing" on the war prisoners in 1950. In his article (September 1950) which blared the headline of the Miami Daily News, Hunter later wrote a book which described how the Red Army of Mao Zedong used terrifying ancient techniques of manipulation to turn or make the people of China into what we can describe as feeble-minded automatons that could be manipulated by the Communists. This crude process is what he referred to as "brainwashing." Hunter explained that brainwashing is a process that changes an individual's mind radically turning this individual into a living puppet or rather a human-robot that does not have the atrocity to be visible from the outside. However, this inflammatory rhetoric discovery by Hunter didn't have immediate impacts until it was experienced three years later during the Korean War. During the Korea War, there was the manipulation of the American soldiers captured and made war prisoners. It was evident when these soldiers began to confess crimes that they did not commit. Specifically, this brainwashing was seen in 1952 when Colonel Frank Schwable was captured and detained by the Korean forces. In February 1953, Colonel Frank Schwable together with other war prisoners were manipulated and had to give false confessions that America was using biological warfare against the UN war requirement on the Koreans which affected unsuspecting civilians. Furthermore, at the end of the war 5,000 war prisoners out of 7,200 captured prisoners ended up making crucial decisions involving petition to the US government to accept and sign their confessions of the crimes alleged on them. Things were even worse when a total of 21 American soldiers refused to be repatriated back home.

The American public became shocked and the threats of brainwashing became very real. Despite the US military denied the charges mages against them by their soldiers' confessions, they were not able to explain how these soldiers were coerced into making such confessions. Besides brainwashing, what can really explain or describe the behavior portrayed by the affected soldiers? Following this, the idea behind mind control became common in the pop culture and this saw the release of movies like *The Manchurian Candidate* and *Invasion of the Body Snatchers* which basically tried to show how outside forces can wipe and control people's minds. There were also several types of research on this topic and in 1980, the American Psychiatric Association tried to carry out researches linking brainwashing and dissociative disorder when dealing with mental disorders. Many Americans went ahead to ask whether the Soviet Communists and the Chinese uncovered a method or machine that was used to rewrite or change men's minds and supersede/replace their own free will. This called for ways with which it manipulation/brainwash could be combated.

All these events in the 1950s were misunderstood. By this time, military studies did not understand psychological torture. Instead, military directors decided that these soldiers needed to be rehabilitated. It was even more devastating when the military directors made an outrageous conclusion by saying that the soldiers were simply weak. They failed to understand the real impacts of brainwashing but instead became worried that their men could not stand up their enemy's torture. The US military then focused on Survival, Evasion, Resistance, Escape program (SERE) which was a program meant to equip military personnel with training in evading capture, torture techniques, equipping them with military code of conduct and survival skills when captured. Most psychiatrists and writers tried to examine and explain the brainwashing basing on "behaviorism which was the most known theory relating to the human mind at this period time. The main assumption behind this theory was that, at birth, the mind of a human is at a blank state and by conditioning that occurs throughout our lives, the human mind gets shaped. The fears of mind-control as a weapon haunted the American thoughts which led to the authorization of psychological experiments. These experiments used biological manipulation such as sleep deprivation and hallucinogens such as LSD to determine if brainwashing were possible. The findings of the research would be adopted in both offensive and defensive mechanisms particularly against their enemies like the USSR.

Psychological Manipulation in Military Culture

Military culture can at times be brought to extreme excesses. It can perhaps be far much worse when prisoners of war are manipulated to turn against their countries or provide false witnesses. Manipulated soldiers can be compelled to slaughter and murder innocent lives. A Few Good Men, a movie acted in 1992 tries to demonstrate how prisoners of war can be manipulated and compelled to murder. Two characters, Downey and Marines Dawson who are marines are faced with murder charges after imposing Code Red. Code Red is hazing that looks forward to correcting the behaviors of an underperforming soldier. Downey and Marines Dawson intended to correct Santiago and this resulted in Santiago's accidental death. These two marines however obtained reduced charges because Jessup, their superior officer gave the order for Code Red. This, therefore, brings a lot of questions. Why would these soldiers carry out their ordered action without murdering Santiago? In order to explain why we have to look at and analyze the concepts behind the nature of subtlety and obedience defining a soldier's decision-making processes. Manipulation of prisoners of war will involve three main methods; authoritarianism, dehumanization and social Conformity based on Lifton's eight criteria for thought reform. Here are the ways with which prisoners of war can be manipulated;

Eight Criteria for Thought Reform by Dr. Robert J. Lifton

1. Milieu Control

This approach involves controlling the communication of information within an environment and within an individual which results in the isolation of the individual from the society. When you are able to control the environment of people and well as what is communicated to them and how it is communicated to them. Milieu Control bases itself on defining unquestionable truths (dogma); coming up with the rules that must be followed when conducting specific activities (establishing protocols), and Making threats or subtle criticisms (the use of innuendo), etc.

2. Mystical Manipulation

Mystical manipulation does not rely on cognitive trickery or social pressures but rather relies on the deeper, mostly overlooked occurrence of wonder (awe) - particularly the overwhelming feeling of powerful zeal that an extra-ordinary event creates. Generally, we can produce awe in many ways; for instance, through a deep connection with the splendor of nature or by being amazed at extreme beauty. Mystical manipulation, therefore, involves the creation of this awe for the purpose of undue influence. This specifically happens when another person has manipulated, created, or rigged the circumstances that force the experience of awe so as to connect the high feeling to something which only they can provide.

3. Demand for Purity.

Demand for Purity exists in high-control groups and our wider culture at large. You will see it in mainstream religions, corporations and even in families. This method takes advantage of the natural human foibles and prays on human insecurities. A total environment divides the world into two blocks. For instance, we have always viewed the world as black and whites. Therefore, each member of these groups is constantly made to conform to these ideologies and always strive to seek for perfection. Here, the power control device is the induction of shame or guilt. This is similar to the cases witnessed during the Cold War. The world was divided into Capitalism and Communism. Prisoners of war from the US were subjected to shame and guilt making them accept the Communism ideologies.

4. Confession

Manipulation is characterized by confession. Individuals will be made to confess their evil thoughts or deeds. These confessions in most cases are conducted in front of other members. The main reason for making people confess is to make it impossible to have secrecy, to abolish privacy and to reinforce the feeling of guilt in a person. For example, Colonel Frank Schwable and other 5,000 soldiers were manipulated to make false confessions.

5. Sacred Science

The doctrines of the group brainwashing its members make its members believe that their ideologies and doctrines are the ultimate truth that cannot be questioned or disputed. Members believe there is no truth outside their group. The group leaders are viewed as supreme leaders who are above any form of criticism. Once an individual belongs to a group that possesses the truth, the individual can; feel more at peace, feel reassured because he/she has found answers to his/her question; and have limited critical thinking.

6. Loading the Language

In most cases, the group likes it when members of the outside world do not understand their language. Therefore, it will use words and phrases that are new or not understood by many. These words and phrases in their way are thought to spoil which serves to alter the processes of thoughts of its members making them align to the way of thinking of the group.

7. Doctrine over an individual

If there are contrary personal thoughts, experiences, or ideas, they should be strongly rejected and if not denied, they must be reinterpreted in a manner that fits the group's ideologies.

8. Dispensing of existence

The influencing group can make a prerogative decision on who should exist and who should not. This at times means that those who are not part of the group are unsaved, are unconscious, are unenlightened and should be converted to the ideologies of the group. Members must reject people who do not join the group. This, therefore, means that the outside world will lose all credibility. Furthermore, any member who leaves the group must also be rejected.

Special Anti-Manipulation Techniques

The Translator Technique

This anti-manipulation technique perhaps is the easiest and most efficient. This technique works like this: Because you already have knowledge in manipulation and brainwashing, suppose you are in a situation where you are being subjected to manipulation by an enemy, you simply translate the verbal and non-verbal expressions by your enemy in a simple sentence. When you notice that your enemy is using manipulation technique, ask them what they mean and if they mean what they are saying.

For example, your friend wants you to attend a party over the weekend but you don't want. Your friend in turn simply says ok but from the look of things, he feels sad and offended on his face. You begin to have feelings of guilt and now you feel like you are trapped. Your desire is not to attend the party, but you also feel bad about your friend being offended and sad. What do you do? You simply use the translator technique. Ask yourself whether you will be breaking your friend's heart by failing to attend the party. Therefore, from this example, it is appropriate that military education should incorporate psychological education that teaches the ways of manipulation. Soldiers must be taught how to identify when they are being manipulated and how to take a firm stand on what they feel is right rather than being persuaded into what they feel is not right.

The Literal Technique

This technique involves making a clear and conscious subtext on the underlying or unspoken message by talking about it. Therefore, you should completely ignore the subtext. Avoid emotional stupidity. For example, you didn't want to attend your friend's party, and he says "it's ok, I understand" but then looks sad and offended. You should ignore the sadness. Prisoners of war who understand what manipulation is should be able to ignore the words or teachings given to them by their enemies. The setup of military prisons is characterized by authoritarianism, dehumanization, and social conformity. This means that prisoners of war can be subjected to anything that will make them conform to the regulations and rules of their enemies. To ignore all these subjections, it requires an individual with very strong will power. Military education should not just focus on Survival, Evasion, Resistance, Escape program (SERE) which equips military personnel with training in evading capture, torture techniques, equipping them with military code of conduct and survival skills when captured but rather should also focus on equipping soldiers with a clear conscious and stronger will power that will not be subjected into manipulation turning them into puppets.

It is clear that the American soldiers of war captured in Korea by then didn't have any knowledge in brainwashing and manipulation. Well, we know that prisons holding prisoners of war are able to make a prerogative decision on who should exist and who should not exist which also can mean that those who are not part of them or their teachings are unsaved, are unenlightened and should be converted to the ideologies of the group, prisoners' lives can be put at risk when they reject these teachings. Brainwashed members can also reject their fellows who do not join the teachings or believes instilled in them. To avoid such threats to life, soldiers can be taught manipulation techniques that will make their enemies think that they are conforming to their teachings but deep down, they are not affected by their enemies' manipulation and rather maintain a clear conscience and will. Combining the literal technique with subtext exaggeration technique can best fit such a scenario. In subtext exaggeration technique, instead of ignoring the subtext, an individual is made to ignore the rest and only react to the subtext. This means that you are not supposed to react to it but instead. Your enemy will definitely expect you to react but instead, without taking action, you choose to openly agree with the subtext and even exaggerate it. This will leave your enemies confused.

The Time Delay Technique

When you feel that you are being manipulated but you don't know how exactly that is happening, you can use this technique. This happens when you are not able to translate the subtext or you are not aware of what is exactly going on, but deep down inside you, you feel you are under pressure and is uncomfortable, it is advised that you should take time to delay and not make a decision immediately. You should be able to take control of yourself and not your enemies. If you are forced to confess some things against your will or rather something that is not true, respond by telling them to give you time think. This will give you time to think more and make sound decisions or confessions.

The Approach to Rinsing Out the Brainwashing

1. Create awareness to the subject that he/she has been manipulated/brainwashed
2. Instead of criticizing or rejecting an individual, it is appropriate that they be aware that they have been brainwashed. However, in most cases, this realization is usually accompanied by anguish and denial.
3. Begin exposing the subject to ideas contradicting the manipulation
4. Make this individual have a broader perspective of the subject that they have been subjected to. Challenge these beliefs implanted in them by their brainwashers.
5. Basing on the new information, encourage the subject to make his/her own decisions

The subject may become anxious at first on whether the decision he is making is for himself or he is just being compelled to make the decision out of shame of making a wrong decision by accepting to be manipulated.

Chapter 7: Cognitive Techniques, How to Use them to Your Advantage

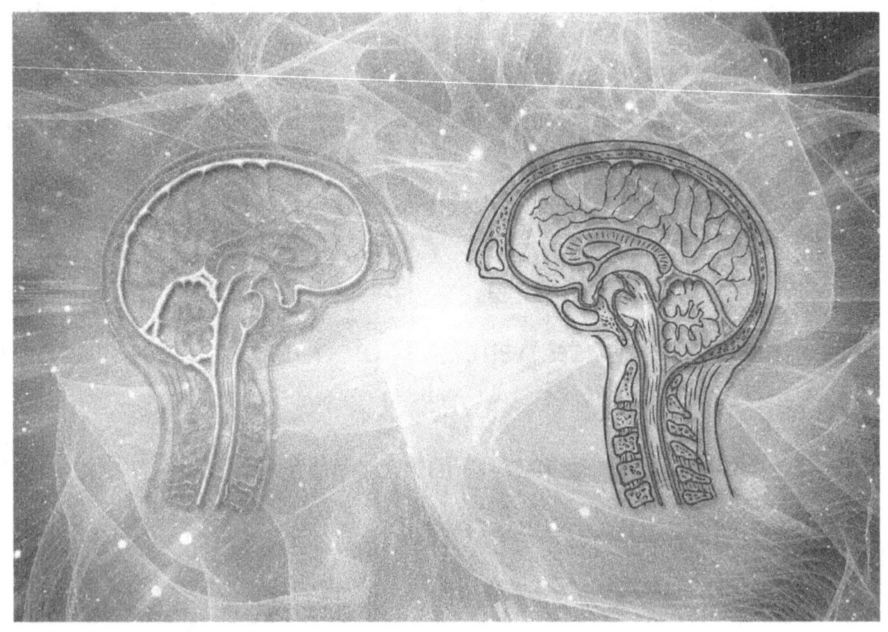

Often when we hear about a brainwashed or manipulated individual, we tend to imagine someone whose mind is being completely controlled. His/her will is being manipulated by some powerful authority which may be evil. In the most extreme cases like extreme cult cases, you will find that leaders can instruct their followers to commit suicide. This was common in Japan, where people would commit suicide as instructed by their leaders. These and many others have made most people believe that it is true that a person's mind can be completely controlled. These extreme cases suggest that humans can be manipulated and can also manipulate others. In most cases, we get acquainted with psychological manipulation during our younger ages. For instance, in a school environment, there is always a schoolyard bully who can be seen as a young master manipulator. Such a child has already learned early that by intimidating his fellow kids, he/she will be able to get what he/she wants. According to researchers, the bullies have brains that exhibit a pleasure response when they see their subjects going through pain. This pleasure is what makes them be addicted to such behaviors of being cruel to others and in doing this; the brain development of their subjects can be permanently stunted.

Two Important Questions About Manipulation

Before we look at the ways with which we can use cognitive techniques to our advantage when dealing with manipulation, we must first ask ourselves these two very important questions;

1. The identification question

This question is concerned with the definition and identification of manipulation. I know you have read this in the earlier chapters but we will do it just to give you a deeper meaning of what we intend to discuss. Therefore, are you able to identify the forms of influence which are manipulative and which are not? To provide a satisfactory answer, we will look at a general definition of manipulation by explaining the diverse forms of manipulative influence. In will also be appropriate that criteria be formulated that will help an individual determine whether a given instance of influence is can be considered as manipulative or not.

2. Evaluation question

This question is concerned with morality. How can one evaluate the moral status of manipulation? Providing a satisfactory answer to this question will tell the morality of manipulation (whether manipulation is always moral or not). A more satisfactory answer will explain why manipulation is immoral. We also need to look at the features of manipulation that make it be considered immoral.

The Answer to These Two Questions

To answer these questions, manipulation has been characterized into three main ways. The first characterization of manipulation looks at manipulation as an influence undermining or bypassing rational deliberation. The second characterization treats manipulation as a form of pleasure; lastly, manipulation is seen as a form of trickery.

1. Manipulation as undermining ration deliberation

In most cases, manipulation is usually said to "subvert" or "undermine" the rational deliberation of a target. For two reasons, this thought can look appealing. First, manipulation greatly differs from rational persuasion. If an individual's behavior must be influenced, it should be done so without engaging their rational capacities. Second, this term manipulation seems intuitive as it describes the forms of influence that bypass the capacity for rational deliberation of a target. Looking at the definition of manipulation as bypassing rational deliberation which introduces non-rational influences into deliberation makes deliberation to be contrary to rational persuasion.

2. Manipulation as Trickery

This approach treats manipulation as a form of trickery and conceptually links it to deception. In both philosophical and non-philosophical discussions, manipulation has always been connected to deception. Looking at manipulation in terms of trickery, we simply mean that manipulation is seen as deception in that it induces false beliefs on a target. Deception is a deliberate attempt to trick an individual into adopting beliefs that are considered as faulty. Manipulation directly influences a target's beliefs, emotions, or desires such that this individual fails to have ideals for self-beliefs, emotions, or desires.

A better way to look at trickery is in Shakespeare's Othello. One character referred to as Iago in this book is a perfect example of a manipulator. Iago uses trickery to manipulate his targets. For instance, through innuendo and insinuation, Iago cleverly arranges circumstance that tricks Othello into suspecting and then believing that Desdemona, his new bride, has been unfaithful. Iago then takes advantage of Othello's insecurities as well as other emotions. This leads Othello into an irrational rage and jealousy that overshadows his love, his reactions, and his judgment towards Desdemona. In this case, trickery relates to manipulation in that Iago manipulates Othello to adopt faulty mental states and false beliefs together with irrational emotions and unwarranted suspicions.

3. Manipulation as pressure

Manipulation can also be seen as a kind of pressure on a victim, forcing the victim to do what the influencer wishes. Basing on this, influencers can use tactics involving blackmailing emotions of an individual and even peer pressure as the techniques of manipulation. The influencers tend to exert pressure on their target individuals by imposing punishments on them in the case that they fail to do what the manipulator wishes. Manipulation, therefore, can be seen as a form of pressure that is neither rational coercion nor persuasion. Concerning pressure level being exerted on an individual, exerting pressure can be seen to fall short of being coercive particularly when here is a continuum between coercion and rational persuasion.

A better example of manipulation as pressure is explained by using rational persuasion into convincing a patient to take some necessary drug by simply coercing the patient to take it. For instance, a physician can intimidate a patient by telling the patient that he/she will be very upset if the patient fails to take the drugs. In such a case, the patient is not fully convinced that the best course is to take the recommended drugs. The patient simply agrees to take the prescribed medication because the acceptance of these drugs is likely to foster a better relationship between him/her and the physician. Here, we see the patient finding it very difficult to resist the proposal made by the physicians. In other words, the authority the physician has in some way exerted pressure on the patient and in turn is controlling the patient.

Using Cognitive Techniques to Your Advantage

Cognitive-behavioral therapy is therapy techniques that are evidence-based and focuses to change the behaviors, feelings, and thoughts of an individual with the goal of improving the overall life of an individual. This leaves the individual satisfied and happy with life. It helps people to identify their thinking patterns that are responsible for their negative behaviors and thoughts. The techniques, therefore, track the dysfunctional thoughts and devices more psychologically and healthier flexible thinking patterns. In most cases, manipulated individuals rarely respond to self-study. They believe in what they have been taught or influenced and will not see anyone criticizing them as an outsider. However, cognitive techniques can be used to slowly bring back such an individual back to the world of reality. Here are the strategies;

1. Assess yourself and identify the problem

The first step towards rinsing out manipulation from an individual is by creating awareness to that individual. Now that you are aware that you have been manipulated, don't deny it, or don't get angry. Try to brainstorm and identify the problem as it is. Write down your beliefs and thoughts. Write down all the things that you think are contrary to the real-world experience. After doing this, try to think about how you can improve your thoughts and bring your beliefs back to normal. Avoid the disbelief that things cannot get better. Critically think, read books and search for solutions that can help you improve your situation that will help in wiping these strong beliefs that deceive you and undermines your rational deliberation. For instance, if you feel manipulated to believe that you are ugly and now you feel lonely, the solution can be by joining some local club where you can interact or even by signing up on some online dating club.

2. Write self-statements that counteracts the negative manipulative thoughts and beliefs

Now that you have identified the main problems as to why you were manipulated or brainwashed, try to come up with ideas that will make you forget the negative beliefs. Try to assess and think about all those negative things or bad decisions you have ever made due to influence; try to identify those tricks and situations with a pressure that have ever made you make bad decisions or take the wrong action. Now that you are aware that you were brainwashed, think of new ways that you would have reacted to such situations suppose they were to occur again. Put them down to counteract your previous manipulated thoughts, actions, and beliefs. Also, note that these self-statements can become too routine. Therefore, ensure that they are refreshed. Just ensure that you translate self-statements into simple language that you can easily speak out. Try to guide your will power by always involving critical thinking before doing accepting something that you feel is manipulative.

3. Find new opportunities to have fresh positive thoughts

Suppose you were influenced at your younger age to have particular negative thoughts or beliefs pertaining to some actions, find ways to replace these negative thoughts and beliefs. For example, there are extreme religious teaches that can manipulate one into thinking that their religion is the best and that those of different religious beliefs are inferior. Such a thought/belief can be replaced by thoughts that all human beings irrespective of their religion, ethnicity or skin color are equal. Cultivate beliefs in you that makes you feel positive about the things that you had initially had a wrong belief on. You can even set your phone to remind you about developing a positive view of the things that you were once manipulated about.

4. Always finish your day by visualizing its best parts

First, put it clear that if your behavior must be influenced, ensure that it should be done without engaging your rational capacities; secondly, note any deliberate attempt by anyone to trick you into adopting beliefs that are considered as faulty;

Lastly, assess through to identify if there was an individual who tried to manipulate you by blackmailing your emotions or by using peer pressure. Therefore, in your journal, write down the positive reaction or actions that you took against any form of manipulation that you witnessed and that you feel you are thankful for. Ensure that you always do this at the end of each day. You can even proceed to share these thoughts online with other people who may be experiencing the same thing. This is a step that will help you create a new association in your mind as well as create new pathways in your thoughts and reasoning. The essence of this is to help you create new ways of thinking and the ways with which you will be viewing the world at large. Make sure that you make worthy decisions that when you reflect, you will feel proud.

5. Learn to accept disappointments

Disappointments are part of our normal lives. The way an individual respond to disappointments affect how quick that individual can move forward. Don't blame yourself when you have been manipulated. Don't be stressed over such issues.

A better approach to this is by allowing yourself to feel disappointed. Have it in mind that in life, there are things that are usually out of our control as human beings. Therefore, only work on what you feel is within your control. It is good that you write down what you experienced when you got manipulated; write down what you learned from that experience and what actions you think will be appropriate to take when faced with such a situation in the future. Assess yourself to determine if you can do it differently and watch out the negative thoughts this experience impacted you. Furthermore, because you already have knowledge in manipulation and brainwashing, suppose you are in a situation where you are being subjected to manipulation by an enemy, you simply translate the verbal and non-verbal expressions by your enemy in a simple sentence. Therefore, make a clear and conscious subtext on the underlying or unspoken message by talking about it. Therefore, you should completely ignore the subtext. It is appropriate that you be an individual who is able to avoid emotional stupidity. When you feel that you are being manipulated but you don't know how exactly that is happening, you can use rely on your thoughts to bring delays on your opponent. This happens when you are not able to translate the subtext or you are not aware of what is exactly going on, but deep down inside you, you feel you are under pressure and is uncomfortable. Take some time to delay and don't make a decision immediately. Ensure that you take control. This is an effective approach that will enable you to move on and in the future, you will feel better. In every decision you make, ensure that it is for yourself and not from being compelled out of shame, pressure, or trickery.

Chapter 8: Nonverbal Communication for Dark Psychology

Nonverbal communication involves what you say with your overall body language without the use of words. Our body language is known to send a strong message to others during conversation. Someone may guess the kind of person you are by looking at your appearance and posture. Sometimes you may say something, but if your nonverbal gestures such as facial expression do not reflect it, others may not believe in it. Nonverbal gestures, therefore, are significant in giving feel and touch to our words. Your tone of voice also speaks volumes about what you are saying and how you are saying it. Both verbal and nonverbal communication is vital, and the gestures we express during conversation are equally important and influential, just as the word we use. Nonverbal cues impact how other people will receive what we are attempting to communicate, and their reaction will reflect how we have delivered the message. If you wish to get a particular response from your audience, on your message, then your verbal communication will affect the kind of a response they will give. In fact, accompanying your words with the right gesture will make you sound more real and believable, and add spice to your conversation and speech.

Body Language and Dark Psychology

When we here of dark psychology, then we think of personalities such as narcissists, sociopaths, psychopaths, and Machiavellians. Sometimes we wish that we can deny them the oxygen of nonverbal communication to minimize their charming ways. Unfortunately, they flourish in dark psychology, and they understand the power of nonverbal gestures very well. They know how to use them to manipulate others to their advantage. They take advantage of the power of body language to minimize their target, manipulate their emotion, thought, and behavior to achieve the ends they seek. Some of the nonverbal cues that they capitalize on are:

- The clothes they wear and how they wear them
- Body gestures such as posture and positioning
- A facial expression such as hypnotic gazing
- Maintaining eye conduct or avoiding it
- Voice, where they raise the tone of their voice intentionally
- Proximity where they manipulate the distance between them and their target

Hypnotic Staring and Gazing

Eye conduct is one of nonverbal skill which is very important in communication. It inspires confidence and shows that you are attentive as the other person speaks. Maintaining eye contact has always been preached an excellent way to make others feel like they are really being noticed. But manipulative people know how to take this vital skill a step further. They set their eyes on you with an intense and focused gaze. Such hypnotic gazing is usually done intentionally for the purpose of testing boundaries. The manipulator often does or says something weird after or before the hypnotic gaze. They then stare at you to test and monitor your response.

In an attempt to lie to you, they may stare at you without blinking much. When someone lies, they usually break eye contact and look down or to the sides. But sometimes they go an extra mile to give a steady and cold gaze to intimidate and control you.

Body Touch and Space Invasion

Manipulative people playfully touch you in an attempt to break the rules and boundaries. They usually do this in a very subtle and charming way. They may reach for your shoulder, peck your cheeks, or touch your hand intimately to see whether you will permit it, especially on your first date. They carry you off the ground when you hug intending to pass a particular message, and test whether you accept it depending on your reaction. They will also invade and violate your personal space to create false intimacy. They do this by leaning too close. Even if you step back, they step forward into your bubble to re-adjust. In this process, they also touch your shoulder or arm repeatedly to try to create rapport.

Constant Mirroring of Your Body Language

This is a famous manipulation technique which dark personalities use to influence their target. At the start, they are trying to mirror you so that they can control you. Later you find yourself reflecting them. This creates trust between you and them and helps to establish a connection that they use to exploit you. The technique is usually straightforward and a basic one, because it only involves copying the behavior of a person. The manipulator takes a close look at your body languages such as gestures, facial expressions, and the tone of your voice. If you are standing with your hands crossed, they do the same. If you are speaking quietly without showing any emotions, they do the same. They do it as carefully as possible to make sure that you are talking in the same way. They also make sure that you won't realize or become suspicious of their behavior when they are mimicking you so that you do not become suspicious.

After some time, you will start feeling connected to them. You begin to behave like them, and that is the time that they realize you are ripe for their purpose.

Nice Dress and Haircut

Dark personalities understand well the power of the first impression. They're physical appearance if therefore the first thing that they bank on. They know the best hairstyle that makes them look good. Your entire outfit will be affected by how your hair looks. One of the things that a person you want to influence will notice is your haircut. When you ignore your hairstyle, you won't look good, and they will know it. Be realistic with your hairstyle and if a particular hair cut doesn't make you look good, let it go and look for a better one. Don't rock around with a haircut that looks terrible on you.

Dress well, without going crazy on fashion if you know you can't sustain it. To impress others, you must be well dressed to create a first good impression. If your dress cannot capture the attention of your target, then they will not pay much attention to you. Those who manipulate others know this, and they spice their looks with flashy clothes and makeup.

Raising Their Voice and Displaying Negative Emotions

This is a sign of aggressive manipulation. They raise their voice when you are discussing something, while in the real sense, they are not emotional. They assume that by projecting their voice high enough to show negative emotions, you will give in to their demand and do or give what they want. They accompany their loud voice with strong body language like excited gesture or raising from their sit to stand on their feet.

Self-Comfort Touches and Pointing

Lying comes with discomfort and stress. The liar then begins to make a gesture aimed at achieving some level of self-comfort. These are gestures such as hair-stroking, playing with wedding rings, rocking, and twiddling. Although we all use gesture often, they increase dramatically for someone who begins to fib. This is when they start to feel that their lie will not go through, and you have discovered their hidden motives. In an attempt to get away out, they may begin to use their hand to point to other things happening around to divert your attention from the matter. If you stick to the topic, they will feel embarrassed and never try to lie to you again.

Micro-Gestures

These are little gestures or facial expressions that flash across one's face quickly. They are hard to see, but experts tend to use filmed footage which they slow down to analyze the body language and hence can recognize them at the middle of the lie when the person is performing it. In real life, these may not be spotted, but you can look for other facial expressions that occur after the liar is done speaking. Either the eyes roll, or the mouth skews as the liar is attempting a quick give-away.

Projected Body Posture

This is when someone stands towering over you. This may happen in the case where the narcissist is physically stronger than you and has a tall and colossal figure. He may lean forward to mask you and inspire fear to diffuse your confidence. He will bring his face closer to yours and look you straight in the face in an attempt to control and manipulate you. He may also stand straight next to you or in front of you, projecting his chest forward to fill up more space and try to minimize you. He may yell at you at the same time to make you yield to his demands and give in to what he is saying or give what he wants.

Avoiding Eye Conduct and Silence

When they are lying to you, and they know that you have realized it, people with dark traits tent to avoid eye conduct. They may begin to look down or blink their eyes quickly or even close their eyes in close succession. Looking to the sides is also another technique used by sycophants to prevent you from getting cues that they are lying to you. They may also remain silent for a while to avoid answering your questions if you have cornered them.

Another time when narcissists avoid eye conduct is when they have silent aggression towards you. If it is in the office, they will get in and avoid looking at your desk to prevent eye conduct with you. They may also greet everyone else in the office and fail to exchange greetings with you. If they exchange greetings, they do so look over your shoulder or looking down to avoid eye conduct. This may be the case when you failed to yield to their demands, or when you have confronted them about their manipulative tendencies which you feel tired of. They may use this silent aggression to see whether you will change your mind and live up to what they want. This may also happen in a relationship.

Fake Smile

A fake smile doesn't reflect the real feeling and emotions. Unlike a genuine smile that involves most of your face, such as the mouth and the eyes, a fake smile only involves the mouth. A smile that doesn't extend to the eyes is fake and may show that you are not reading from the same page with the deceiver. It means that they are telling you something else while their real motives are hidden. A deceiver will often use a fake smile to appear more genuine while trying to convince you to believe in them. By carefully monitoring their smile, you can find out whether it is a real one or a fake one. If you notice a fake smile, be careful, and steer clear of what they are telling you because the chances are high that such a person is not genuine.

Rate and Tone of Speech

Since they aim to control and manipulate you, a person with dark traits will speak quickly and adopt an audible tone, so that they can present so many details to you without giving you time to think. They know that when they allow you time to digest the content, you may detect the exaggeration and the half-truths in the message. Sputtering, without giving you time to respond, makes you get overwhelmed with details. They also know that a tone that is audible enough will make them sound confident and truthful. The aim of all this is to overwhelm you with so much detail before they lay their claim to you. By this time, they know that you are already tired with very little energy to resist. The manipulator then drops the bombshell, and if you are not careful, you may find yourself falling head over heel for the trap. When you confront such a person, and you see their voice beginning to fade and their speech getting intermitted by moments of silence to figure out what to say, then you realize that theirs was a calculated move to achieve a selfish goal at your expense.

Chapter 9: Recognizing a Dark Personality and Dealing with It

If someone, either your friend, colleague at work or your boss tells you that you are a triad, or that you have a dark personality, you may protest vehemently or cringe. This is because the term sounds unfit, and one may say that it should be reserved for crime novels. While that may be true, it is essential to mention that we interact and deal with people with dark personality in life. You may not be a triad yourself, but what about if your friend, colleague, or your boss is someone with dark psychology? How would you recognize so that you can deal with them in the right way?

It is good to understand what dark personality is so that you can recognize triads when you come across then and device the best techniques to deal with them accordingly. With the ability to identify people with dark personality, you will be able to know how they magnetize so that you can avoid falling prey to their antics.

The term dark personality refers to a person who shows little or no empathy for others. Such characters have negative traits and thy display errand and sociopathic behaviors. Due to their negative personalities, they are often misunderstood by others. They are poorly received and accepted by the public due to their questionable conduct.

Kinds of Dark Personalities

1. **Sociopaths:** these are victims of the environment. They behave negatively because they have gone through traumatizing situations. They, therefore, use sociopathic behavior as a defense mechanism to help them cope by responding poorly to sexual or violent situations.

2. **Narcissists:** these have exaggerated levels of self-esteem than other people. This inflated sense of self-importance makes them infallible to themselves and end up lacking empathy for others. Due to their unhealthy self-love, they are proud and have no tolerance for criticism. They manipulate others and put them down for their gain. They also have no empathy for others. Just like any other character trait, narcissism varies in strength from one individual to another.

3. **Psychopaths:** this is a dark personality where a person tends to display harmful characteristics towards others. They have a distinct brain difference, and their brain may show some

damage, especially the insula, cerebral cortex, and frontal lobe. Since the frontal lobe controls a person's ethical conduct, such individuals display psychopathic behavior if it is raptured by something. They become explosive and controlling. They have no remorse and often display anti-social behaviors.

4. **Machiavellianism:** individuals in this category display extreme manipulation traits towards others. They condone cunning habits and deceit to further their self-interest agenda. They have no morals or feeling for others, and they will take lying to new heights to achieve their hidden motives.

Signs of Dark Personality

- **Manipulation:** people with dark personalities tend to have manipulative tactics such as lying for their gain. They will deceive anyone so that they have their way. By spewing blatant lies, false accusations, and spinning the truth, they will ultimately distort your reality.

- **No long-term friends**: when you dig a little deeper, you find that people with dark personalities have no long-term or a real friend. The only connections they have are casual acquaintances, nemeses, and some buddies the trash-talk.

- **They lack empathy:** one of the hallmark traits of dark personalities is lack of empathy. They don't know how to identify with other persons' feelings. They never do emotions that belong to others. They can't make you feel seen or accepted.

- **Flatter:** shady characters may use buttering words and butter you up to ask for favors from you.

- **Lack of morals:** they will hurt you and show no remorse. They even go ahead to make callous, thoughtless, and derisive comments and remarks. They knock you down with insults, call you names, hit you with hurting one-liners and make funny jokes that are not quite funny.

- **Boastfulness:** this trait stands out in individuals with dark personalities. Because they mostly have low self-esteem, they find it difficult to accept other people being ahead of them or doing better than them. They end up talking of themselves and their achievements most of the times to push themselves up. Their goal is to lower other people's esteem so that they can boost theirs because that makes them feel powerful.

- **Cynicism:** they are always thinking of the worst and have a hard time seeing the positive side of anything. They, therefore, tend to shoot down any attempts to progress since their view of the world is somehow jaded.

- **Psychological entitlement:** they have a deep belief that they are superior to others

- Sadism: they have a desire to inflict physical and mental harm on others for their pleasure and benefit.

- **Egotism:** they are preoccupied with their achievement at the expense of others. They also have a desire to boost and underline they're own financial or social status. They do this to make them feel smarter and better than everyone else, as it helps them create an illusion of being self-assured.

- **Spitefulness:** they have a willingness to retaliate and cause harm to others. They will even accept to be disadvantaged so that they can see another person suffer.

- **A deep need for excessive attention and admiration:** They feed off other peoples' compliments and need a lot of praise. If you don't give it readily, they will fish for it, so that you can tell them how great they are.

- They are preoccupied with fantasies of ideal love, beauty, brilliance, power, and unlimited success.
- **Social classism:** they believe that they are unique and special, and should only associate with other particular or high-status persons or institutions because they are the ones who can understand them.
- **Envy:** they are full of resentment, but they defend this by always saying that others are envying them.
- **Always right:** they think they are right about everything and they never apologize.

The root cause of all these traits is what is called the D-factor. This is the tendency where one seeks to maximize their utility at the expense of others, and it is usually followed by beliefs that serve to justify such tendencies. The motivation behind all dark personalities is the tendency to put oneself before others and try to justify such behavior in all manner of rationales.

A person's D-factor may manifest itself as psychopathy, narcissism, or any other trait that is associated with dark personality or sometimes a combination of either of them. It may also show up in various dimensions of life. It can manifest as extreme violence, duping, rule-breaking, and using deception antics in the public and corporate sectors. In such cases, the knowledge of an individual's D-factor plays a useful role to determine the probability of the person to re-offend or to get involved in more harmful behavior.

Studies also show that the dark triad of psychopathy, narcissism, and Machiavellianism go hand in hand most of the times. This dark triad acts as an adaptive mechanism, where traits are seen as a strategy that seeks immediate reward and gratification, which result in survival and reproductive benefits for the person.

The Attractiveness of Dark Personalities

Narcissism or psychopathy are never considered desirable traits. Nobody would want their friends or partners to have such qualities. However, we often find ourselves being mysteriously drawn close to people with such personality traits. Vampires seem to be the symbols of sex, and girls who are mean are the most popular in school.

Recent studies have uncovered that people with dark personalities are attractive and more appealing physically than others. They succeed well in making themselves attractive with flashy clothes and makeup. They, therefore, end up being popular than anyone else at first sight.

A study was carried out where information on students' personalities was collected beforehand. These students were lined up to introduce themselves briefly to others. After the brief, students completed surveys about the first impression made by each student who had introduced themselves. Students who were perceived to be more likable had scored higher on narcissism. This is because they had a flashier appearance, more attractive facial expressions, and confident body language. That means people with dark personalities have some skills, which they use to carry and present themselves in an engaging way that impresses others immediately at first sight.

This initial appeal of dark personalities is hard to resist. There is always a general assumption in us to associate physical attractiveness with a host of other positive antics. This is called the halo effect. When we are physically attracted to someone, we also tend to think that they are kind, honest, and empathetic. Therefore, creating a veneer of physical appeal gives people with dark personalities a favorable first impression. Exploitive characters are more successful at combining physical attractiveness with humor and confidence to lure others into liking them at first sight.

People with dark personality traits are also experts at keeping their dark side hidden. However, their appeal and physical attractiveness begin to count for nothing after sometimes when they cannot hide anymore. After several weeks or months, their popularity begins to decline. With time people get wiser with their ways and start to avoid them. Most people will shy away from engaging in long term relationship with them since the hallmark of their trait is only interpersonal manipulation and exploitation. That is why you should always be slow to form your judgment when you meet someone for the first time.

How to Deal with People with Dark Personalities

Individuals with dark personalities have their ingenious ways to have their way. Learning to extricate yourself from the clutches of dark triads is therefore essential. This is especially in corporate or public sectors where volatile, arrogant, and domineering traits can disrupt teamwork and interfere with performance. Although there is no magic pill to accomplish this, there are steps that you can take to develop their strengths, neutralize their unsavory behavior, lessen their negativity, restore team harmony, and enhance productivity.

Coping with Anger

People with dark personalities have difficulty managing their anger. A good example is a person with psychopathic traits who is likely to be prone to hot-temper and aggression. If a team member is showing these traits, then such a situation needs to be defused with speed. Sign of moderate anger such as sweating, flushed face, and raising one's voice are easy to spot. But some people may suppress their passion, and express it in passive and aggressive ways such as ignoring people and sulking.

You need to employ the right strategies depending on the type of person you are dealing with; whether they show normal anger or suppressed anger. If you feel threatened, then you need to stay safe by temporarily leaving the room depending on the way the situation is. Distance yourself emotionally from someone's behavior if they are showing a sign of ongoing suppressed anger towards you. Don't take their behavior personally since it is not about you alone. By employing the right techniques, questioning, and active listening, you can try to identify the cause of their rage and counsel them accordingly about their behavior.

Dealing with Bullying

When anger spillover, it translates into bullying. Bullying will be characterized by threatening behavior and verbal abuse. It can also escalate into spreading malicious rumors, unnecessary criticism, or belittling someone. To deal with bullying traits, you need to confront the bully. Hold them accountable for their behavior by being assertive on them and standing your ground. Also, give the necessary support to the victim of the bullying.

Spotting Manipulators

You can influence people at work, using several ways. A team member can be more inspired to be more productivity through encouragement and praise. But for a person with Machiavellian tendencies, he may try to selfishly manipulate co-workers by influencing them through deception and coercion.

Manipulative people tend to be good at concealing their antics and actions. You can spot them by looking at specific signs such, as repeated excuses for one's behavior which is often hurtful, someone who doesn't take no for an answer or someone trying to get different people to serve his purpose by presenting a different face to each one of them.

Confront such manipulators with their specific actions and let them know how such actions are causing harm to others. Be clear and assertive that they must change their behavior and make an agreement with them so that you can make them accountable in case they cause more hurt in the team.

Coping with Narcissism

The selfish nature of a narcissist is less of a threat, but more of a headache, and it can head up disrupting the harmony and the morale of a team. Due to ego, a narcissist will do everything possible to grab the attention of all the other team members, and put herself in the spotlight. She will dominate essential meetings and discussions and demand credit for ideas by talking of herself as the sole achiever in the whole team.

As soon as you realize something like that, you must raise it with her immediately because she may not be aware of the harm she is causing to others. Be prepared to stand your ground and meet her demands or claims with solid counter-arguments as people with such big egos never expect to be questioned or challenged. Put her in a position where she will need to cooperate and depend on other colleagues so that she can learn to be understanding and respectful.

Build the Skills You Need to Cope

Some of these behaviors are difficult to deal with and manage, especially if you lack the confidence to deal with conflict. By learning to be assertive, you can improve your skills in dealing with conflict. Also, you can focus on developing your ability to understand others and know their perspectives and emotional state. Enhance your skills for dealing with people through emotional intelligence and empathy, and always be aware of the message they are trying to pass to you through their body language. Use emotional intelligence to manage your emotions better, and understand others if they cannot understand you. With these skills, you can easily spot unbecoming behaviors in your team or in other people and device the best strategy to deal with them.

Avoid Contact Whenever Possible

This is the strategy that most people use to deal with these negative characters. If you get to the point where you can't tolerate their antics anymore, and you feel that you have done your best coping with the situation, distancing yourself from these characters can be the only way to avoid their manipulative behavior. Use text message or send emails when you want to get in touch. Remember that people with dark traits are really charming, and they rely on their presence and looks to have their way. One study revealed that people with dark traits succeed more when they get a chance for a face to face negotiation. Avoiding physical contact may, therefore, be a great way to extricate yourself from there charming physique.

Chapter 10: Case Studies: Learning Dark Psychology from Real Events

The core of dark psychology is to manipulate people to achieve specific pre-determined goals and objectives. The science of manipulation date back to many years. Since then, knowledge has always been used to manage and control people. Manipulation works, only a few recognize it, a few minds it, and the majority play along. In this chapter, we are going to look at case studies of real events that reflect the art of dark psychology and how it has been used to control and manipulate people.

Case 1: Kings

In the early days, kings used to sit on thrones. These were built taller than the average chairs or set on a pedestal. The aim was to make the king appear tall and massive than everyone else. This was meant to manipulate the people to perceive the king as the dominant figure, and symbol of power and control. Palace and castles, together with their inner chambers, were built very tall. This was once done intentionally to make people approach or enter inside to feel small and reduced to insignificance.

In some monarchies, the entrances were built so low that for anyone to enter, they had to bow and stoop. This was meant to humble anyone who came there since bending or stooping low is known to be a sign of humility and respect.

Case 2 Theatres

These are halls of performance. They have a long-standing history of manipulation. During concerts, a considerable number of paid audience members are planted strategically among the attendees. This fake audience is trained in giving direction to the crowd. They are supposed to instigate the crowed into reacting to the performance by responding appropriately at a particular time.

They usually train to follow the performance carefully, and they know the right time to activate the crowd to respond appropriately. When it is time to laugh, they are the first to do so. When it is time to shush others, they are the first to do so. When it is time to applaud, they are the first to do so, and when it is the right time to give a standing ovation, they are the first ones to stand. This happens so often during different events, performances, and ceremonies.

Unknown to the audience, they end up following suit, clapping, and shouting themselves dry, without knowing that they are being mirrored to do that. The audience has always followed the cues of performance, since forever until now.

Case 3: Advertisements

Every advertisement aims to manipulate us into thinking that we can't do without the product. It is no secret that companies will go to great lengths to make it appear as if it is your idea when you purchase their product. They have spent, and still, continue to spend vast amounts of money to understand the psychology behind consumer buying behaviors. They then use this information to come up with the most successful advertisements and predict new trends to get us to buy and continue to buy their products and services. These misleading ads are planned meticulously to manipulate us based on psychological findings that are studied by marketers every day. Advertising psychology runs deep, and companies know how to take advantage of celebrities and situations to make huge sales.

For example, there was a huge billboard which was being used for advertising a particular body lotion for women. In the billboard was a celebrity with the most coveted figure which every woman craves for. The superstar had extremely smooth skin and was 95% naked so that his body shone on the billboard clearly. She had been pictured with the sexiest smile that will melt the heart of a lion while applying the lotion all over on her body. The product being advertised was then placed strategically beside her with the lid open to make it look as if she was using it in reality. Then the words "100% Natural product for 100% Natural skin. Feel me now!" were written beside the picture and the lotion. The billboard was then strategically placed outside the CBD where it was to capture the attention of everyone going to or coming out of town.

First, the company chose a well-known celebrity who had a following on social media, and since she was a famous musician. The purpose of placing her there naked was to draw attention, and adding the word "fee me now"! was purely to manipulate the thinking of customers. It was reported that many males bought that product for their wives and children just because of that sexy smile of the woman in the picture. Although the celebrity was paid for the work, it might be true that she never uses that product! But as a result of her being associated with the lotion, many people headed up buying that product, due to her social status in the society.

Another example is eHarmony, a well-known dating site. It had an ad, where the founder boasted that the site had successfully aided millions of people to fall in love, and find their partners on the site. The statement then ended there without proof of whether such couples existed in reality. It was a manipulative statement because it ignored many things. Did those who fell in love on the site stay together? Did they end up in marriage? Did the eHarmony partners beat the well-known fact that most marriages end up in divorce?

The actors used on dating sites are cross-checked to make sure that their looks are above average. If they use actors whose looks are below average, which is common in everyday life, maybe the sites will not have many followers.

There was an ad which was used by BMW to promote the sale of their products. In the background, the ad had a picture of the BMW. Then there was a tractor, and a lady dressed on G-string and bikini with one leg lifted to step on the side of the tractor. Then the words "Test Drive Her Now" were cleverly inscribed on the ad.

Such advertisement was purely manipulative. The first question you would want to ask yourself is, "What does the lady in the picture dressed in G-string and bikini have to do with the tractor or the car?" Then the other question is, "What are you test driving? Is it the lady or the car?" even the text itself is manipulative. The aim is to capture your attention, feelings, and emotions to the extent where you cannot resist the sale! The ad achieved that by making so many buyers think of the car in terms of a woman.

Case 4: Relationships – Personal Story of Jude

I come across an app that people use to meet new friends, who can later evolve into possible partners. I was fresh from another relationship where I had been heartbroken, and I wanted to forget about the heartbreak as soon as possible. Out of curiosity, I gathered my courage and signed up. Before long, I attracted the attention of one guy. For this story, I will call him Jack. Jack started off with kindness and complimented me. My pain was numbed by the affection that Jack had shown to me, which I needed badly. Though I was still heartbroken, at least I had found someone to nurse my pain. At that time just I wanted to hear someone telling me that I was beautiful and amazing because I had somehow lost confidence in myself after the heartbreak. After continually talking for two weeks, he solicited me to be his girlfriend. Since I felt that I was done with my previous relationship, I agreed without a second thought. I was not sure whether I was over my X, but I wanted to use this as a way of compensating for what had happened. I knew that he would be incredibly jealous when he realizes that I was with someone else.

After being with jack for one week, I said to him that I'd be going for a youth club ball in the coming week. I explained to him that I wanted to go and at least have fun with my peers since I had already paid. He became full of range, described the whole thing as teen disco, and said that some other guys would start to seduce me there and end up cheating on him, and in case it happens, I will have myself to blame. He said that it would be my own fault, and I will carry my own cross! I was so confused. Though I wanted to attend that event, I began to doubt myself. What if Jack is right? If I refused to heed to what he had told me, I thought that I would be so disloyal. I even began to think that it is one of the reasons I was dumped before because maybe my former boyfriend had felt that I'm a player. I was afraid of being portrayed as the wrong person so early in my new relationship. He blackmailed me by saying that he loved me so much, but I didn't love him back equally. Though it was just one week of being together, I panicked and told him that I loved him too.

Eventually, I attended the event since I had already paid the money. For the whole time I was there, Jack kept on messaging me, telling me that I was horrible and that I was a cheater who cannot be trusted. He went ahead and called me, but there was so much noise in the event, and I could not hear him at all, so I had to hang up. My hanging up worsened the case. He hurled insults on me via text messages until I began to feel guilty about what I had done. I ended up leaving the event, excusing that I was sick because I had already panicked. When I left the game, jack was very happy, and he cooled down.

But, although I was exhausted, he could not let me sleep. He wanted to keep us talking on the phone, and when I hung up, he would guilt me up. I had to comply since I was afraid of appearing bad to him at such an early stage of our relationship. I tanged along. No matter which day it was, he used to call me every day in the morning for a long time without wanting to respect my work schedule. If I told him that I wanted to prepare myself for work, he would complain that I seem not to have time for him and that I wanted to talk to someone else.

I had no option but to stay on the call until he was ready to leave for work. I would then prepare myself quickly and rush to work, sometimes without breakfast! I become sick of it with time because sometimes I would even get late to work because I had to talk to him in the morning. Sometimes I also used to rush without being well prepared to avoid getting late and lose my job. I began to ignore the morning calls, but he would continue to call until my phone run out of charge. Any time I did hang up, he would call again after five minutes. Later, when I reach for my phone, I would get so many disparaging text messages, telling me how unkind, uncaring, and horrific I was.

I would feel guilty and awful, but when I try to explain to him about the work schedule, he did not want to understand me. He insisted that I should never refuse to receive his calls no matter what. The relationship became so overwhelming, and it drained me mentally, emotionally, and physically. At work, he used to make a Skype call to me anytime I was free, especially during tea time and lunchtime. I would take my tea and lunch while talking to him. Sometimes, he would even call me during important sessions when I was talking to a client or in a meeting with my bosses. It was very embarrassing.

He would then accuse me of being seduced by my male colleagues at work anytime I was unable to pick his calls. He didn't want me to go to another application when we were on Skype because it would block the camera. He was continually monitoring me at work. I never had the freedom to call my colleagues or text them because he would accuse me of cheating, and being insensitive and uncaring, no matter how I tried to prove myself innocent. He wanted me to send him pictures of where I was and who I was with, anytime I went out with friends. He would call me regularly during such occasions.

In case my phone went out of charge, he would use my friend's phone to call me. He manipulated me to do away with any guy in my Instagram and Snapchat because he branded them as risky, saying they may turn against me and beat me up. Since I was emotionally weak, I got scared and complied. I had no time to argue because I felt depressed, and an argument would worsen my condition. I lost my confidence and became a victim of his manipulation.

Soon, he turned his manipulative tricks to my friends, when they disagreed with him about his controlling habits. I also thought that he was protecting me as he had always said. He distanced me from them saying that they would destroy our relationship.

I had given him my pins to everything, including the bank. When I tried to refuse, he would tell me that I was hiding something, and my commitment to our affair was doubtful. I found no fault with this, since I felt that it was for the sake of our love, and being open to each other. One day he read a group chat where I was conversing with my friends.

I had commented positively on a picture of a guy that one of my friends had shared in the group. when he saw it, Jack scolded me by saying that I was looking at another guy. He said that such groups would lead me into cheating on him. I began to avoid them, as well as cutting off some of my friends. To me, Jack was always right, and I could not dare correct him because he would insult me and go silent on me for days. Sometimes, he would turn violent and slap me.

After six months, I went for therapy because I become stressed and depressed. I overcame the depression, gained my confidence, and regained my emotional strength. I realized the truth that I did not need anyone to confirm my beauty and tell me that I was terrific. I realized that Jack was my greatest obstacle towards realizing myself because he only served to worsen my depression from my previous relationship. I broke up with him immediately. I blocked him in all my social media accounts and changed my phone number.

My friends and family helped me to cope with the situation. I came to realize that they were the people I should have listened to. I had given Jack too much power to control my life, and steal my emotional independence. You should always be careful because manipulative guys take advantage of your vulnerability to achieve their hidden motives.

Conclusion

Manipulation has been used to control people by governments and religions since time memorial. The reason why government and churches manage us is because they are always using specific knowledge behind the scenes to manipulate us so that we can believe in their agenda and ideals. Manipulation can be negative or positive. When someone uses emotional and communication skills to help you change for better, then such manipulation can be regarded as positive. But when people who flourish in dark traits use manipulation techniques to further their own interests at the expense of others, then that becomes negative manipulation.

Today, whether we know it or not, we are being manipulated from all circles. In the workplace, some colleagues try to use dark techniques to further their own interest at our expense. In our relationship, some partners may take advantage of our vulnerability to manipulate us. In the mainstream media, we are being manipulated and influenced by all sorts of advertisements. With everyone trying to reach for us and gain some mileage on us in one way or another, it is good to learn to be on the lookout so that we can be able to sift between those who have good intentions of helping us and those who are out to hurt us.

Usually, people who use deception techniques and controlling attitudes on us have bad intentions. Such a person can be either a psychopath, sociopath, narcissist, or Machiavellian. These are people with dark personalities, and their central agenda is to instill fear, through intimidation so that they can gain control of us and use us as a means to achieve their hidden ends. They have dark traits such as lacking morals, egoism, cynism sadism, lack of empathy, and many more. When you notice such characteristics in your colleague, partner, or friend, then you should exercise caution when they try to use the charming ways or emotional blackmail to corner you.

Such people usually use fear and deception to exercise superiority so that they can take advantage of others. Generally, manipulators are full of ego and only thinks of themselves. He will go to any length to get what he wants for himself and doesn't care about hurting others. It is tough to change such people because they have low self-esteem, and inner insecurities drive their lives.

They don't take advice or criticism. Learning to cope with such people is also crucial since they are full of anger and rage, especially when you go against them. When you see their range moving out of control, you can leave the room immediately to ensure your safety, and come back, later on, to engage them in the right way. Their behavior at work should be tamed since it can lead to disagreements in teams and affect teamwork negatively.

By investing in developing the right cognitive, emotional and communication skills, we can be able to recognize when people are trying to use manipulative techniques on us and deal with them head-on before their manipulative behavior spirals out of control.